"Mr. Lyden's book is very informative, precise and up-to-date. His book warrants a review by all Workforce Development professionals who help Veterans deal with the challenge of employment and making decisions. Additionally, I would advise Veterans to purchase, review and share the book with other Veterans."... Rick Parker - CMSgt-USAF (Retired)

"I am an Infantry Company Commander by trade, but currently specialize in helping wounded, injured, and ill Soldiers transition from active duty military service to the civilian world. I have read "Veterans: Do This! Get Hired!" and personally endorse it as an exceptional resource without hesitation. If you know a Veteran or Service Member who is planning on exiting the military, please recommend "Veterans: Do This! Get Hired!" It is a short read and functions more as a handbook than a self-help guide. Don't let your next interview turn into an ambush by walking into it unprepared. Take the time to read this one."...Brett D. Kelley, CPT, IN, Commanding, K CO, 1-12 IN, 4IBCT, 4ID

D0939225

HonorVet.org a company Co-founded by Senator John McCain's son Jim McCain, and a fellow Marine Jesse Canella, Co-Founder and CEO, endorsed the book and said: *"If you're a veteran you need to read this book!! Best advice for getting hired that we have ever read."*

"I was blown away by the depth of his [the Author Mark Lyden] knowledge and solution based information is an understatement. If you are a Military Veteran or Active Duty Service Member making the transition, YOU NEED this book NOW before someone else steals your dream job."... Mr. Todd M. Hecht, Veteran and Co-Owner and Managing Partner of Military Stars (www.MilitaryStars.com)

"Thoroughly enjoyed reading the publication. Your insight to helping educate our returning vets is remarkable."...Gene Clark, Veteran and Director, Military & Veteran Enrollment Services, Rochester Institute of Technology

"I am a returning Iraq veteran with disabilities...The information is straight forward and easy as hell to understand. I followed his advice in chapters 2&3 to the letter. I saw immediate results on the same day I posted my resume by getting 3 requests for interviews. Mark is on- target with this information. I wish this had been around when I first ETSed."...Matt K., U.S Army (Ret.), Panama/Iraq/Somalia

"For months, my job search had become a process of trial and error. This book put the deluge of information I've found on how to search for a job in an easily understandable priority. The book is straight forward and you don't feel like you're spending your valuable time reading. I strongly recommend this book to any veteran or longtime professional. Veterans: Do This! Get Hired! Has given me a new-found confidence."...E. Wallace, Veteran

"You rocked during the interview! Can't wait to do it again!!"...The Keating Network Radio Interview (www.keatingnetwork.com)

"Thank you so much. The information you gave was very informative."... Alvania Frazier, CBS Radio/WPEG-FM, Producer

"Mark was great at spotlighting the benefits of his book and I was impressed, until I read it. You see Mark was holding back and being humble. His book is one of the best guides I have seen for helping anyone, not just veterans, get hired. Every vet should have this book."…JW Najarian, US Veteran Group, NetworkingFools-Fools Media Group, CRE Professional Investor Group, CRE Distressed Assets Assoc.

"I picked your book up twice. The second time tonight I read it all the way through. It was hard to put it down. I can see how your book needs to be read by all veterans seeking jobs and those getting ready to go back to the civilian world"…Bob Calvert, Host, (www.talkingwithheroes.com)

"I have read Mark's book and it is very good. A great starting place for veterans looking for work..." Ted Daywalt, CEO of VetJobs.com

"I finished the book in less than a week. This is the best book I have read in the last year referencing military transitions into the civilian market. Mark said it perfectly about resumes writing, job interviews, and job fairs. Veterans: Do This Get Hired is by far the best book out there for the military transition personnel"… Dorothy Woods, U.S. Army, 23 yrs.

"The book ... was designed to educate. It's written in plain and simple English, with nothing fancy; no big words; nothing to intimidate; nothing to slow you down. Just solid information and guidance from someone who 'knows.' Simply put... if you want to up the odds of getting hired, read the book. It's worth the money and time, neither of which is much expense. Enjoy!"… Bob Schecter, Founder at Florida RealMarX, Principal at Networking Fool, Principal at DMI

"I find that oftentimes the job search candidate is inundated with so much informative job search material they lose site of the purpose, which is to land a job! In my opinion, Mark Lydens' book cuts to the chase and presents precisely what is needed to successfully land a job in a most focused no nonsense fashion."… Roger H. Siegrist, Director, Human Resources for Conrail

VETERANS: DO THIS! GET HIRED!

If you're a veteran and need a job, or if you are in the military and about to transition back into the civilian work force, this advice may be the only thing that will help you get a job in this challenging job market.

PROVEN Advice to help you get hired!

by Mark Lyden
A Professional Fortune 50 Recruiter
www.DoThisGetHired.com

ISBN-13: 978-1456496128
ISBN-10: 1456496123

Visit www.DoThisGetHired.com to Order Additional Copies.

Contents

Acknowledgements

To all veterans and service men and women around the world: My family and I truly appreciate your great sacrifices in keeping our country safe and protecting our freedom. Thank you.

To Jesse Canella, CEO / Founder of HonorVet (HonorVet.org) I sincerely appreciate your great enthusiasm and support of this book and the personal time you spent with me throughout the process. I am honored to be a part of such an important and noble cause.

To the entire HonorVet organization and all those working there, thank you for supporting this book and giving me a chance to help vets in a significant way. I sincerely appreciate the opportunity to be part of this great cause of helping vets find jobs.

To all the veterans that helped with this book. Your comments, thoughts and advice have been invaluable. Thank you for your time and great feedback.

To my wife, Kat: Thank you for your patience and help with this book. You're mine and I'm yours and we go through life together with our dogs. What a great life it is.

INTRODUCTION

What Qualifies Me to Give You Advice?

Decide the value of my advice for yourself.

US military personnel right now are facing a perfect storm: veterans are coming back from Iraq, Afghanistan, and other combat areas, only to have to battle again to get a job because of the economy—and because they don't know the best ways to transition into a civilian job.

I can help.

I'm not going to waste your time regurgitating points from other books or from off the internet. What makes my book different is that it teaches vets how to get hired from the point of view of an experienced, actively practicing, professional recruiter.

Over the past two decades, I have:

- been a lead recruiter for a Fortune 50 Department of Defense (DOD) contractor for close to 15 years

- recruited for small, medium, and large-sized companies.

- recruited for Secret and Top Secret programs, and I have held a Top Secret Clearance for many years.

- interviewed and screened thousands of candidates.

> *Who better to teach you how to get the job you want than the person who evaluates potential employees for a living—an experienced Professional Recruiter?*

- created seminars and presented to over 10,000 jobseekers from coast to coast.

- designed and taught classes on the best methods of Resume Writing, Interviewing, How to Work the Job Fair, Negotiating Salary, Applying Online, Cover Letters, and many more.

- mentored hundreds of employees and prospective candidates.

- headed or participated in well over 150 different job fairs and expos across the country.

- led many minority recruiting events.

- conducted or aided in recruitments at national conventions and symposiums along with national, regional, and local recruiting events affiliated with dozens and dozens of academic and professional organizations.

- recruited for the majority of technical and non-technical fields out there at all levels.

- been responsible for negotiating potential employee salaries.

- hired or helped in the process of hiring thousands of candidates at all levels.

- trained, advised, and mentored well over 100 different people on how to recruit great people, including vets, and the techniques to do so. I have taught engineers, business people, executives, new hires and even interns on recruiting methods and processes.

I continue to do all these things today, fulltime, *in this economy*, so I know what vets must do to get hired. Now, with all of this experience, knowledge, and success, I want to help *you* learn the inside story behind how veterans get hired. Whether you're in your twenties or fifties; whether the position you seek is technical or non-technical, what you'll find in these pages will give you a significant competitive advantage over those competing against you for the same job you want.

Though I could have probably written a separate book on each of the major topics I've included in this one, the fact is, you'd probably find that much information overwhelming. Besides, why would you want to spend time sorting through *good* ideas, when I can provide you with the *best ideas; the ones I have seen work most often and are the most successful with getting people hired?*

> **Sure, other books are longer and list hundreds of things for you to try...but this book contains only the strategies that work best to get veterans HIRED.**

The information here will provide you with the most profound and immediate help possible; these are the tips, tricks, secrets, and techniques that I have seen work most consistently for veterans seeking jobs.

I know what works and what doesn't because this is my profession. I see what gets people hired and I see what doesn't. I study and analyze what other company representatives are doing and saying as well as what is happening in the job market. This is part of my job and for me to be successful at it; I need to know what other hirers are doing. This attention to detail has helped me consistently hire the best candidates year after year. I have been so successful at it I have been asked to teach other recruiters how to do it.

So what does this have to do with me helping you get a job? Simple. I know so well, what companies look for, when screening or evaluating a candidate, I can teach you exactly what to do and how to do it so they take notice. The first step at getting you hired is to get their attention and there is no better way of doing that then to give them what they are looking for.

Anyone telling you that their way works all the time is lying. If one method worked all the time, then everybody would learn it, and there wouldn't be a need for this book or all the information that is out there on the Internet. However, my experience recruiting in today's market gives me a unique perspective on what gets people hired and that will help you.

Advice and Good Advice: A few years ago, I was at a public library, where I noticed a small display of books as I entered—all books about how to get a job. I picked up a book by some Ph.D., opened to one section, and started to read.

I was surprised by what he was telling the reader. Yes, some points were correct, but others were totally off base. Plus, it took him about 10 pages in each chapter just to get to the point. Then, when he did, the point was incomplete. I read further and began to get irritated. This Ph.D. wrote this book to help people get a job, but half of what he said was incomplete or downright wrong. I found myself saying "No," in my mind as I read, and then I was saying it out loud! (Then I looked up to see if anyone had heard me…and a few had!) The point is you should be getting advice from someone who understands this challenging market; someone who works in it. Anyone with seemingly good credentials can give you advice but that doesn't make it good advice.

I have read or reviewed many of the other books and many of the websites out there that attempt to give vets and other candidates advice on conducting a job search. The advice given is not always good and too many times, it is just completely wrong. This is one of the reasons why I decided to write this book.

The process that leads to getting hired is inherently a soft science, mostly based on opinion. Most books cover the standard topics like interviewing or resume writing, and the authors tell you what they think will work. For example, there is debate out there about having an "Objective" section on your resume. Some say you must have it, others say you shouldn't have it. My advice is when you are applying or interested in a specific job, you should have it. It just makes good sense because not only is the "Objective" section one of the first things a potential employer sees on your resume, it is also a chance for you to immediately and clearly convey to them that it is your goal to get this specific job. In this book, I'm telling you about what I *know* works.

Here is another example. From my experience, I know most hiring managers want to get the candidate count down to a manageable number and then move on from there. One of the easiest ways of getting the count down to this manageable level is to simply eliminate those without a particular keyword or phrase on their resume. Sure they eliminate a lot of great candidates that would have been excellent at the job but they don't think that way. They are thinking they have a lot to do and they need an easy way to reduce the resume count down to a manageable level. There are many other ways that I see vets getting themselves automatically removed from the list of potential job candidates—most of them having to do with mistakes they're making on their resumes and in their online applications—but I have you covered with a chapter on each. After reading them, your entire view on what your resumes and online applications need will completely change. You'll be *very* surprised.

MY DEAL WITH YOU, THE READER:

Your life will change, if you follow the advice in this book. That is a bold statement but the reason I am comfortable in making it is because I have seen it happen with thousands of people. Having a good job that you enjoy doing is a life-changing thing, and I know if you follow my advice in this book, this will be the case for you. So, if I help you with the advice and information in these pages, I would really appreciate it if you would: (1) Share this book with another vet, and (2) Simply let me know how my advice helped you. My e-mail address is Mark@DoThisGetHired.com. If you have a suggestion on how I can make this book better in the future, please let me know. Remember, most of the techniques, tips, tricks, and secrets you are going to read about were developed from my experiences with people just like you. I want to hear your thoughts and experiences dealing with what you have read in this book. It is important because what you may share with me may be able to help another vet.

Chapter 1

Why Is The Transition So Hard?

The Challenges in Your Transition from the Military to a Civilian Job

Yes the transition from military to civilian life is hard.   Many things make it hard, and some of these are things that only you and your fellow veterans can understand.   One thing is clear, however--acquiring a good job is critical to making a successful transition to the civilian world.

Unemployment is just too high for veterans.   According to Honorvet.org it is about *21 percent*.   That fact really got me motivated to write this book.   I have wanted to contribute or give back to the men and women who served our country and this was the perfect opportunity for me to help.

Those getting out of the military, no matter how many years they have put in, are finding it very challenging to find a job.   Also, because so many soldiers coming back from places like Iraq and Afghanistan are electing to leave the service, the problem is that much bigger.   It is nothing short of a crisis.

Together, however, we can change that for you.   My advice has helped thousands get hired, even in this difficult job market.

This book is not a long book, as you can see. It's not meant to give you every possible angle or piece of information that might possibly work. That is just too much information for any reader to take in without ending up overwhelmed with the task of trying to learn all of it.

And the fact is you *don't* need to learn all of it.   In addition, I also believe in the law of diminishing returns which means there is a point where more information just doesn't benefit you very much and is not worth the effort. The vast majority of vets only need to learn what works best—what gets company representatives to notice them and to want to hire them.

What this book will give you is what has been *proven* to work—what has been proven to get people hired. It will not give you a hundred different interview questions that a company might ask. It will not give you multiple ways of approaching a company at a job fair or event. Simply put, what you'll find in these pages is the method and process that will give you the best chance at getting hired.

Please understand there is a ton of information on the internet about what you should do when looking for a job. People giving advice to vets probably have the best of intentions but fall short when it comes to providing information that can mean the difference in a vet getting hired or not. I often look on the internet too, just to see what information is out there. I can honestly tell you, 50% of it is just wrong. This is why you must consider the source of any advice or information you decide to use.

In my nearly 15-year career as professional recruiter, I have seen hundreds and hundreds of vets with the same problem; once they get out of the military, they can't get hired. But over the last few years with so many service men and women doing their duty and then electing to leave the service, the problem of getting vets jobs is huge.

The problem I have learned by talking to vets is that they feel they just can't get the attention of employers. They apply and apply and they just can't get someone to call them; to interview them. Then that makes them feel as they are unwanted or that employers are not interested in them. It's not true.

First, you need to know that getting noticed and getting companies to call you back is a problem for everyone. From those in college to those that have 20 years of experience in this job market everyone is having that same problem.

Now, I know what you are going to say, "If everyone is having the same problem, then why is unemployment for vets significantly higher than the national average?" The answer is simple: civilian employers are programmed to look for certain things. They have a script to follow, a script that helps them to sort through the vast majority of job candidates…which are *civilians* and NOT vets. They look for people that simply match or follow the script they have developed, people who give them what they are looking for. And you know what? Almost every vet I have met and asked about how they are approaching finding a job, seem to have one thing in common. They just don't give employers what they are looking for in the way they are looking for it. In other words, what vets say and how they say it doesn't match the script that the companies are using to find employees. Let me explain further:

As you know being in the military, whatever branch of service, is a unique experience. The military has its own way of doing things. It has its own processes, methods, and techniques to get things done and make decisions. *The military has its own unique language.* And you know what? Companies are the same. They look for certain things when looking for future employees. They watch for those things, and simply pick people that have most if not all of what they are looking for. And here is the problem for vets: They don't speak that language.

> *As you know being in the military, whatever branch of service, is a unique experience. The military has its own unique way of doing things.*

For example, when you are at a job fair, did you ever wonder how company reps can talk to a candidate for three or four minutes and decide if they want to take that candidate to the next part of the process? Well they are looking for specific critical things and you either show them you have those things or you don't in that short period of time. They are looking for specific language that indicates you match with them. Or how about when a potential employer looks at a resume for under ten seconds and puts it in the "yes" or "no" pile. Again, they are looking for specific language you use in your resume so they can decide. If you have it you go into the "yes" pile. If not, well you are in the "no" pile.

I have seen it time and time again. When two vets meet, the language they use and the way they address one another is significantly different than when two civilians meet. For example when two vets meet there is military rank to consider. There is branch of service to consider. There is division and even base location that enters in the conversations. Yet, most of the conversations I have seen between vets seem easy and natural. I believe that comes from many things. A common respect. A common goal. Perhaps a set of rules on how to engage one another or a familiarity of being part of something that is in common with one another.   Maybe it is just a common bond.   Yet it is very different than the way two civilians meet one another and communicate.

Can we agree that those getting out of the military are used to the military way? They are used to following orders and doing things the way the military has taught them to do it.   They are *familiar* and even *comfortable* with the military way of life because that is all they have known for a number of years.   So in any given situation, vets are most likely to rely on what they know the best—what has worked for them in the military.

This is the problem.   This is one of the main reasons why the unemployment rate is higher for vets. Those vets coming out of the military simply do not know the approach that works the best when trying to find a job or getting hired in the civilian world.   Vets just don't know the processes, methods, and techniques that will get them noticed. They don't know the language.

Now, some vets may know some of the civilian approach or language but the problem comes when they have to sustain that throughout their job search process.   Often what happens is they use what they know in some parts of the process, but when they are not sure, they revert back to what they know the best, the military approach. That does not work, and that is what prevents them from getting hired.   Let me give you an example.   Let's say your resume is really good and you are at a job fair. It is your turn to go up and talk to the company representative and for the three or four minutes you are talking, you just do and say everything right; you spoke their language.   Now they schedule your for an interview.   But the interview is longer and many questions.   After the first question, you just revert back to what you know the best and that is the military language.   You start to use acronyms like POV and PX to describe a situation where you got in your own car and went to the store. Well, you lost them.   Now they are thinking you are not going to be able to communicate with non-military people and they hire someone else.

You want to know what makes it so hard for vets when they have to compete for the same jobs as civilians? They have to totally learn a new approach; and new language. Civilians don't. All they have to do is adjust their approach or language so that the potential employer will see what they are looking for and hire them.   In other words, it takes a little more time and effort for vets because unlike civilians they are out of practice.

This is where I can help you. It is time not only to level the playing field, but to give vets an advantage. I know what companies look for specifically. I know how they want information presented. I know their systems, their motivations, and their fears when they are considering hiring someone. The funny thing is? It is not that complex. For vets to succeed, it really comes down to them having an easy-to-follow process in each major section of their job search that not only makes them stand out to the employer in a positive and unforgettable way, and makes it *extremely difficult* for an employer not to give them a job offer.

For those readers who are engineers or technical people, it's important to keep in mind that even for technical positions, the process of recruiting candidates is not like a mathematical equation where you simply follow the steps and get the right answer. There are a significant number of "soft" skills like psychology and communication involved. The brightest minds in Human Resources (HR), Psychology, Talent Acquisition and other fields have tried everything to make recruiting more objective; to take the soft skills like opinions and feelings out of the process. But the fact still remains that no matter what has been done, no matter what methods or processes have been implemented, evaluating job candidates is still, and will always be, largely a subjective process—no matter what the psychologists and hiring professionals may want to admit.

> *Your ATTITUDE is the most important attribute a professional recruiter looks for. It is more important than Military Experience, Leadership, your GPA, ANYTHING.*

For example, when going to a job fair or career fair, have you noticed that the majority of the recruiters behind the booth seem to be Human Resource (HR) or non-technical types? Want to know why? Simple. Again in general, they are better at the soft skills than the engineers and technical types. They are better at the subjective side of the recruiting equation or evaluating according to the set scripts or processes we talked about earlier. (That said, some of the very best recruiters I have ever worked with are engineers or technical people; however, they were able to learn both the objective and *subjective* side of recruiting, and this is such a rare ability that there are very few recruiters like that out there).

An employer's choice to send non-technical types to represent the company at a job fair makes perfect sense, since the vast majority of initial candidate interviews are behavioral in nature. Amongst recruiters, they're most commonly known as *behavioral* or *structural interviews*.

Why is that? Because the *right attitude* is the most important attribute you can have. It trumps everything else. The most critical item when being evaluated or interviewed is your attitude.

Why? Think about it from the interviewer's point of view. What do you think is the biggest fear a hiring manager has when hiring a candidate? Some might assume that it is hiring someone who is unable to do the work. But that's not it. In my experience, hiring managers are most fearful of hiring someone with a bad attitude. Why? Because a bad attitude often has a viral effect that negatively affects the whole team.

Bad attitudes cause conflict. Conflict lowers morale. Lowered morale decreases efficiency. Inefficiency translates into lost time and money…which is misery for guess who? The hiring manager.

If hiring managers hire employees that can't do the work, they have a fighting chance to work around it by sending the new hire off for training or giving them different assignments that they can fulfill successfully. But having an employee with a bad attitude is nothing short of throwing a psychological grenade into the middle of the room with all team members present.

Moreover, if a candidate with a bad attitude gets hired, who do you think gets the blame? You're right: the recruiter or person that recommended them. So wouldn't it be logical for a company to send out those people that tend to be the best at screening for this relatively subjective, very soft-science attribute we call attitude?

The professional recruiter's mantra is, "Once you know they have the skill and experience, hire for attitude." That's why you see mostly HR and business types out doing most of the initial screening.

Lastly, many of the vets that I have talked to (especially the ones that did tours in Iraq, Afghanistan, or other combat zones) feel as if some employers may consider them as "damaged goods" in some way. Most vets that I have talked to don't come right out and say it directly, but it's a shared perception among many of them. Some vets feel that employers will think they might call in sick more than other employees because they are having trouble adapting to civilian life. Others feel employers think that vets in combat zones might not be able to handle the pressure of their work and schedule because of what they have been through.

Look, I'm not going to lie to you and say that no potential employer is ever going to think this, but you can't prevent it. You can't force people to think (or not think) a certain way. However, you want to know what helps alleviate this perception by those *very few* potential employers that might feel this way?

It's simple. Show them that you are a great candidate who matches their job so well that they *must* consider you. Yes, it is that easy. Employers are wired to find the best candidate for a particular position; it's their prime directive. If you present yourself as that candidate, (which includes having a great attitude), the vast majority of employers will take notice, and your chances of getting a job offer will rise exponentially.

How do you present yourself as that "best" candidate for a particular job? That is where I come in to help, so let's get to work.

Chapter 2

Resumes

Included are 4 Quick Tips to help you stand out in a positive way.

What can I possibly tell you about writing your resume that has not been written about or cited on the internet or in almost every, "How to Write a Resume" book? I even hesitated to put this section first because you, the reader, might think this is going to just be a review of what you already know or have read 1,000 times before.

It won't be, I can assure you.

> **The way most vets approach their resume writing is completely OBSOLETE. Did you know the structure of your resume is equally as important as the content?**

This is a short chapter by design. It is meant to give you 4 Quick Tips on improving your resume that most vets don't know about and yet are very effective. Most importantly, this short chapter is the foundation we will build upon for the next chapter, "Applying Online." That is where I teach you an extremely effective way to get employers to notice you from out of a sea of candidates that have applied for the same job. So let's get started.

Resume writing as most vets know it and practice it today is obsolete. Yes, there are still some good books out there that give you valuable information. And for the most part, career advisors or professionals do a good job at giving you the basics of putting together a good looking resume.

But, in reality, there is a paradigm shift in how to prepare a resume, and few people have seen it or are talking about it. In reality, resume writing is now married with the online application process. They go hand and hand and it is critical that you understand the relationship between your resume and how you should be applying to jobs online. Like I stated before, I will go over the entire online process in the next chapter; however, to keep things in some logical sequence, we will start with resumes first.

Very early in my career, I used to subscribe to the belief that when evaluating a resume, the substance or content was the most important thing, and the structure or format was a distant second. That seems very logical. After all, if a candidate had great leadership experience, great work experience, or even great grades in school, etc…who really cares about the location of the information on the resume as long as it was there? Well, things have drastically changed in the past few years with the advent and dominance of the online application processes. Now, the structure or format is *equally* as important as the content or substance. I could even put up a strong argument that the structure is more important than the content. This might sound counter intuitive and some who read this might even characterize this as being ridiculous but it is not. There is clear logic not to mention proven performance (people getting hired) to back this up. I'm confident by the time you get done with this chapter and the next one, "Applying Online" you will see my point clearly. But first you need a good, solid resume to work with.

If you are starting from scratch with your resume, my advice is simple. Go to a career professional and pick up an example of a good resume or even ask a friend who has had a professional look over theirs to give you a copy. Then, create one just like it with your information. That should be considered your "Base Resume." Like in constructing a house, this is your foundation that you build upon. If you already have a resume and have gotten it checked over already, use that as your base resume. This is the resume you should only hand out to people for general purposes like at a job fair or if someone asks you to send them your resume.

Now, take that resume and see if you can implement my 4 Quick Tips below. These tips have been proven to help vets stand out in a positive way by making it easy for employers to see what they are looking for.

Plus they help illustrate your strengths in a way that allows employers to see how great you really are. Too many times, I have met a vet, looked over their resume and talked to them, only to discover that their resume doesn't even come close to representing how great they are.

QUICK TIP #1:
Count Your Hours

Most of the people I know, unless they have been in the military, really have no clue how many hours per week military people put into their work, so you should mention it. When you are explaining your experience on your resume and what you were responsible for, make sure you put in something like, "Worked an average of 60 hours/week." The reasoning behind this is simple. It helps educate the person reading your resume on how many hours you actually work as well as to convey to them that if there are occasions where a 60-hour workweek is needed to get something critical done, you have experience in putting those kinds of hours in, and you're up to the task. It is comforting to an employer to know that you have that kind of experience, stamina, and can-do spirit.

In addition, some vets or current service members take a class or two while performing their work assignments, as well as juggling family responsibilities. This is nothing short of impressive to employers because it suggests to them that you value learning, are motivated, are willing to work hard, and can manage your time effectively.

Why is that important? Because these are common and critical attributes that they hiring professionals look for in potential employees. The easiest way to work this into your resume is usually right after your title for a specific job; that is, usually under the "Experience" heading. It doesn't have to be a long explanation; it can just be something simple like "Average hours of work per week: "60" or just, "60 hours/week."

Or if your Experience section lists a particular military assignment, and during that assignment, you took 12 credit hours toward your degree or to further your education, you should state that along with the assignment, again, just after your title. It might read something like, "60 hours/week, while taking 2 college courses/year."

QUICK TIP #2:
Numbers and Symbols Are King

This is a short tip, but a powerful one. Employers love to see experience with numbers attached to it. They want to see your accomplishments in a way where they can come to the conclusion that you will do the same for them. This is why you should always cite things like: Percentages (% increase, % decrease, % change), Time Saved (how many hours were saved per week, per month, per year), Money Saved (Cost Savings per week, month, or year), Number of People reporting to you (How many people you are in charge of).

Now, when you use these numbers, you should always write them out in numerals and the appropriate symbols such as "160% increase in performance," or "80% decrease in paperwork needed." Some might say this is grammatically incorrect, but it is completely acceptable to do this on a resume, and it is very effective in drawing the employer's attention to the very accomplishments that are most likely to impress them.

Another example is money. If you are glancing at two resumes and one says, "one hundred thousand saved" and the other says, "$100,000 saved," see how the numerals pop out at you? Use this tip and incorporate as many numbers into your resume as you can. Also, when you are putting numbers in, it is always good to use the largest numbers

> *Employers love to see experience with numbers attached to it. They want to see your accomplishments in a way where they can come to the conclusion that you will do the same for them.*

you can work into your resume. For example, instead of saying that you saved "5 hours/week for 15 weeks," you should say that you saved "75 hours over a 15-week period." The bigger the numbers are, the better it will get their attention.

Here is a great trick: many people make the mistake of putting time saved on their resume, but never follow it up by what that equates to in money savings; which is what really gets employers attention. Here is a simply formula to do that. For example let's say you implement an idea that saves, like the example above, 75 hours over a 15 week period. Take that 75 hours and times it by what is called the "Burden Rate." The Burden Rate is the hourly cost that it takes to employ one worker. It includes things like health benefits, pension, 401K contributions, really every expense that it costs a company to employ one employee for an hour.

For example purposes let's say the Burden Rate is $100 an hour. Well, you saved 75 hours, so you times that by $100 and you get a total savings of $7,500. That is what you need to put on your resume. Now, if you don't have a clue as to what the burden rate is, find someone in the finance department and simply ask them for it. They may tell you they can't give you the exact number, but if they can give you an approximation, that is fine for what you need. Remember, the goal is the show numbers, and especially money saved. Corporate America loves that. It really grabs their attention.

QUICK TIP #3:
List Your Years of Work Experience

There is always a debate out there on certain topics in the job hunting process. Having an Objective section on your resume is one of them. Instead of boring you with the sides of the debate, let me just tell you: Yes, you should have an Objective section on your resume.

One of the main reasons is that an Objective section lets you set the tone of your entire resume quickly. The Objective is always the first thing on your resume, so it is the perfect opportunity to state two critical things. The first thing is what you want, and the second is how many years of experience you have. So for example: "A full-time Project Management position where I can utilize my 8 years of experience." This immediately tells the reader of your resume exactly what you are interested in with their company, and how many years of experience you have. Years of experience are almost always a requirement of the job, so stating these two things in an Objective is perfect. Now you have the employer in the mindset of what level you will fit into the company if hired. In other words, it automatically qualifies you for the experience level of the job and says that you are a mid-level person. That is what you want them to know right way.

If you don't have an Objective section, normally people have their experience listed in some kind of chronological order. All that does is make the person evaluating your resume have to do the math of calculating how many years of experience you have. Now, some would say that this is no big deal, and they are probably right, but my point is you took the time to write a resume that has one goal. That goal is to get you put into the yes pile as quickly as possible. Having an Objective written as I've suggested gives potential employers what they want to see, in the way they want to see it, quickly.

To put it another way, if you were a hiring manager looking for a project manager with seven to ten years of experience, and you had to review 100 or more resumes to see whether they had eight years in Project Management experience, wouldn't you agree that if somebody clearly states in their Objective that they want a Project Management position and have eight years of experience, you would tend to pass someone into the "yes" pile? Remember, people screening resumes initially take only a few seconds to look at each one. I know, because I do it almost every day. Believe me, you want an Objective section.

MUCH BETTER THEN THE RESUME: Not too long ago, I was at a job fair. I was working the booth, and a woman approached me wanting to change jobs. It was lunch time, so I had a little more time to spend with her since the line was not long. I read over her resume. It was average at best, but nothing really exciting. I asked her if she had applied online yet, and she said no, so I went into my script about how she needed to apply online while looking over her resume a little more. Then I noticed that she worked at a hotel. I had no one waiting, so I started to ask her about that.

You would not believe what I discovered: she worked 45 or more hours a week at this hotel, managing all the housekeeping staff. She did this while attending school fulltime, with more than a fulltime load of credit hours each semester. She told me how she was paying for her entire education herself with no help from anyone. Sometimes, she would be called in late at night to resolve a dispute or to fill in for someone who didn't show, and then she would go right to class with no sleep.

Obviously, this woman was nothing less than impressive. I granted her an interview the next day, (she had to take an hour off of work to do it and asked me if it would be ok if she could come in her work clothes but offered to dress in a suit. I, of course, told her there would be no problem with her wearing the work clothes!)

The next day, let me tell you, this woman was the best interview of the day. She had great examples and stories to share as she answered the questions I asked. Then, after the interview, I spent another 15 minutes with her, helping her fix her resume using what I have just told you in this chapter. *Wow.* What a difference those fifteen minutes made.

The point of this story is her resume didn't represent her well at all. It didn't give me her story accurately. It didn't convey the great experience she had, nor did it represent the level of dedication or all the sacrifices she made to get her education. She was nothing more than an average candidate on her resume, but in reality, she was extraordinary. Her new resume got her a lot of attention, and she was hired soon afterward.

QUICK TIP #4:
List any Clearances Separately

This is important: Before you show your resume to anyone, run it by the security department in the organization that got you that clearance. This is very important to make sure the way you show your clearance on your resume is appropriate.

For those of you who are fortunate enough to have some kind of security clearance, make sure that your resume has a separate heading that says, "SECURITY CLEARANCE." Then, list your clearance.

Too many veterans have some kind of clearance and either fail to list it or bury it in the text of their resume somewhere. This helps show that you have something most people don't have, and this separates you from the pack. It also makes it easy for the employer to see that qualification; again giving the employer what they want to see. If the position you are applying to has a clearance requirement, they quickly see you have it, and you go into the "yes" pile. If the position does not have a clearance requirement, separating it out so they can see it gives them a general sense that you are trustworthy and honest or you wouldn't have gotten the clearance. So either way it helps you.

Chapter 3

Applying Online

Ignore this, and chances are you won't even be considered. Learn the 7 Critical Steps that will give you a significant competitive advantage.

In the recruiting world, it is now being argued that a candidate's ability to strategically navigate the online application process is the *most critical* part of their job hunt. I'm not a 100 percent there yet, but I'm close. The facts are there are more people getting hired off the Internet than through all the recruiting events and all the professional recruiters combined. I see nearly every large, medium, and even small companies now having some kind of online employment application process on their website. At job fairs and recruiting events, I consistently and constantly hear company reps instructing candidates to apply online, because that is the only way that they will be considered.

Why do you think the vast majority of companies ask you to go and apply online? If I didn't know and I was reading this, I would probably say something like: "Who cares? Can you just tell me what I have to do to get noticed?" But having a true understanding of why so many companies are adamant about you applying online will help you understand why you have to do it a particular way. After all, you don't want to get lost in the abyss called "Applying Online" like most do, right?

There are a few good reasons why companies want you to apply online. The obvious one you already know: it's an efficient way of collecting and tracking a talent pool with little to no touch labor. That saves money. I would agree with this.

However, in the predominant motivating factor for corporate America is *fear:* fear of litigation and liability. You see, if you are a big company and it can be shown that you didn't treat someone the same as everyone else or that you were not fair in the hiring process, you leave yourself open to, potentially, a very expensive lawsuit. Having some kind of system in place that treats everyone the same and doesn't discriminate among applicants whether they are male, female, black, white, Hispanic, or whether their first name is Bill or Saddam, means that no one can be accused of discriminating against a candidate for gender or race or anything else. This reduces liability, which is the goal of corporate America.

For small companies, the liability is even greater, as a single discrimination lawsuit could potentially cost them their entire business, so no matter what the size of the company, limiting risk by insisting upon online applications is a sensible move.

So here is the big question: *Why is this important for you to know?*

The answer is if you understand the motivations behind why companies do it, you are on your way to understanding how you can leverage that to your benefit.

> *Applying online is nothing more than a test of your ability to match the language in your resume with the key words and phrases in the job description to which you are applying.*

You see, there's a downside for hiring professionals when the whole system is set up that way: the more generic the application process is, the harder it is for us to spot exceptional candidates. And remember—hiring the best candidates possible is what we get paid for. Sure, we can look at something like the number of years of experience someone has. But what if the job calls out for someone to have eight to ten years of experience, and one candidate has eight years and the other has nine? Both meet the experience qualification level, but should the person doing the hiring assume that the one candidate with nine years' experience is the better candidate just because of that one extra year? Of course not.

So how does the hirer knock 100 applicants down to the five they want to interview while still treating everyone equally? They simply use the computer to search all the resumes for certain key words and phrases from the job description.

It is very similar to a Google search. The hirer enters in a word or phrase and hits the enter key. If your resume has that key word or phrase, you stay in contention. If not, you are out. Some systems are more sophisticated and give a percentage-compatibility score for the candidate.

So that's the game you're playing. Look at the key words and phrases used in the job announcement, and be sure to use them, as often as possible, as you list your Objective and your Job Experience. Then, create an Interest Areas section at the bottom of your resume and list the key words and phrases that you just incorporated into your resume again to give you a better chance at raising your percentage of compatibility. This gets your resume a higher rank, and gives you a better chance at getting considered by the person with hiring authority.

The mistake that the vast majority of vets make when they apply online is that they follow the directions blindly without knowing what I have just told you. That is why so many outstanding veterans complain to me about how they have applied to twenty jobs and have never been contacted even once for any of them. I tell them, "Well, you're doing it wrong. Don't follow the directions!"

How are you ever going to get noticed?   Remember, they want everyone to do the same things, apply the same way, so that everyone is equal, and they can just pick people by a very impersonal process…so no one can yell foul.

DO IT THIS WAY: The 7 Critical Steps

Before you apply to any job opening, before you set up any account or profile on any website, before you do *anything,* wouldn't it be nice to have the inside story on what the manager is looking for in a candidate— the required skills or knowledge they want you to have—so that you can highlight them on your resume?   Well, you already have that information in the job description, and here is how you use it and the best way to apply online. Here are the 7 Critical Steps:

    1.   Before doing anything else, go to the company website and print out all the jobs that interest you.

2.   Take a highlighter and highlight the key words and phrases the manager uses to describe what skills and knowledge he is looking for right from the job description.

3.   Take the key words and phrases you highlighted and incorporate them throughout your resume.

4.   At the bottom of your resume, create a heading on your resume called "INTEREST AREAS," and take all the key words and phrases you highlighted and list them under this heading.

5.   Then, set up an account online, taking those same key words and phrases and incorporating them into your profile or the "interest areas" section they ask for.

6.   *Then* apply for the jobs.

7.   As you apply to more openings, continually update the key words and phrases in your resume, in your profile or interest area section.

This is known as *reverse engineering* your resume. From the job description, see what the employer wants first. See what are key words and phrases are that they want to see. Then adjust your resume and apply. Just remember, to do it right, it will take you about 40-45 minutes to take your "base resume" and transform it into a resume specifically for each job.

Remember to approach it this way, as if each job that you apply to is the *only* job your resume is geared to. It may sound like a lot of time and effort, but for you to stand out and get contacted, your resume can't just be a good match, but must be a *great* match. Reverse engineering is the way to ensure that that this is the case for every job you apply to.

ONLINE SCREENING PROCESS

Now, I can't tell you what key words and phrases an employer is going to use. But you need to incorporate those key words and phrases verbatim, because you never know how sophisticated their screening process is.

Often, even at very high-tech companies, the screening process is actually pretty primitive. You have a person sitting in front of a computer, and it is her job to screen resumes. Now, you would think that the person chosen for this job would need to be able to understand the difference between, for example, an Industrial Engineer and Mechanical Engineer, or between Finance and Supply Chain Management. And many of them do...but a significant amount may be a little unclear on the differences. And some screeners, frankly, don't have a clue. So how can they screen resumes? Ironically, as they prepare to do their initial evaluation of a batch, they go through virtually the same process I just told you about: they just look at the job description and simply note the key words and phrases the manager used, type them into a field on the computer, and press "ENTER." Then whoever doesn't have those key words or phrases in their resume, exactly as the manager typed them, is simply counted out.

Here's an example: Mechanical, Aerospace/Aeronautical, and Civil Engineers often use computer software called Finite Element Analysis to find weak points in a structure's design. In the engineering community, it is commonly known by the acronym FEA.

> *Use the 7 Critical Steps, and you will have a far better chance at getting to the next stage in the process.*

So, let's say you are an FEA expert. You have years of on-the-job experience with it. You teach it to others at your company. You've even taught advanced classes in FEA to master's candidates at the local university. In fact, you are widely considered one of the top 10 FEA gurus in the country. And now let's say you find a job opening on a company's website that says they need someone to do FEA full time. This is your perfect job, and you exceed all the qualifications. In her job description, the manager has written, "Must be expert at FEA."

A perfect fit, right? But let's say that instead of calling it FEA in your resume and online application you call it, "Finite Element Analysis."

Guess what: your screener may not have any idea what FEA means, so he might just type "FEA" in the field and press enter. And you know what? You may be counted *out.*

Isn't this crazy? Why should you be counted out just because the person screening the resumes doesn't have a clue?

It's not fair, but it's the truth in many companies, and now that you know the truth, you can use it to your advantage; now you have a step up over similarly qualified FEA experts who don't know to use the exact wording from the job description. Outmaneuver the computer screening process so that you have the best chance at being looked at. I'm not saying lie or cheat. I'm just saying to completely cater your resume to every job you apply to. Use the **7 Critical Steps,** and you will have a far better chance at getting to the next stage in the process.

A Possible Hitch, and How to Avoid It

When I teach seminars on this topic, a student will often ask, "Won't they look at my resume and count me out when they see that I just listed all the key words and phrases in the 'Interest Areas' section?"

It's a good question. They might, especially if you haven't first incorporated those same key words and phrases throughout your resume.

That is why *doing both* is critical. For example, just incorporating the key words and phrases into your resume is great and might get you through to the next step, but it might not raise your percentage compatibility to a high enough level, causing you to miss the cut-off. Remember, with the online processes being the way they are, there might be ten candidates that by luck score a higher percentage compatibility, and although you meet the all the qualifications, these ten others will be considered "more qualified" according to the computer, and you'll be counted out. That is why having the "Interest Areas" section helps: it helps boost your compatibility percentage. Moreover, if you just cut and paste all the key words in the "Interest Areas" section without also incorporating them into your resume, they *will* notice see this, and count you out.

Now, when I say, "incorporate the key words and phrases into your resume," what I mean is, have them distributed throughout your resume. Change or add bullet items in appropriate places. Change your "Objective" to include some of the terms in there. The more time you spend on doing it this way, the more calls you are going to get.

Try the 7 Critical Steps. They have helped get thousands hired. They will do the same for you.

Finally, if you follow these steps, are applying to jobs online, and find that you are still quickly getting counted out, that usually indicates that you're not doing a good enough job catering your resume to each specific job. If you find yourself in that situation, go back to the 7 Critical Steps and follow that advice step by step. Remember, when you are applying to a particular job, your resume should be entirely focused on just that one job.

I've seen candidates try to speed up the process, and when they do the 7 Critical Steps, fail to tailor their resume for the one specific job they're applying to. Let me give you an example: Suppose you are interested in a Marketing job that is posted on a company's website. Now, marketing is one of several fields you are interested in. Others may be Project Management, Accounting, or Procurement. That's great. But even though you've used the 7 Critical Steps on your resume and have an Objective section, your Objective reads,

> OBJECTIVE: To obtain a full-time position in Project Management, Accounting, Procurement, or Marketing where I can utilize my 8 years of experience.

This is *wrong*. You're applying for a Marketing position, not for anything else. If I'm the person looking at your resume, I would say to myself, "Well, this is a Marketing position, and it seems as if Marketing is their last choice and they would rather do Project Management, Accounting or Procurement." Then I would put your resume in the "NO" pile.

Look, it's ok to have other interests in other fields. It's ok to apply to different jobs that are totally different skill areas. But when you are applying for a Marketing job, your resume should be focused on nothing but marketing and the skills that are involved in marketing. Sure it's ok to have some of your other skills in other areas listed, but the focus should be on selling yourself as a marketing person, not as anything else. Getting back to the example above with the way the Objective was written; it's wrong because it should only focus on marketing. This is how it should read,

> OBJECTIVE: To obtain a full time position in Marketing where I can utilize my 8 years of experience.

If you use the 7 Critical Steps and you are counted out before anyone even contacts you, this is your signal that you have to do a better job at focusing your resume just for each job you apply to.

Chapter 4

Job Fairs

Includes 3 Huge Tips that could, on their own, get you the interview.

So why is going to a Job fair so important for vets?   After all, most of the time they feel as if they stand in line (sometimes 30 minutes, especially with the larger companies) just to talk to a company representative who then basically tells them to go apply on the website. What a waste of time right?   Wrong. Look, when you boil it down, the Job fair is a chance to be seen; a chance to impress a company recruiter or representative enough so they will take you to the next step in the employment process. Yes, the odds are not in your favor when there are dozens of other candidates in line trying to do the same thing; at least not until you read this chapter. But let's approach it another way. Let's break it down to what I like to call, "The Prime Directive," or the one main reason for attending a job fair.

My job here is to transfer your stress. Most vets, especially in this job market, go to a job fair with the stress of performing well enough just to get one interview with one company. I can't take away that stress, but hopefully, instead, I can transfer it to you being stressed over the fact that you have many interviews with multiple companies.

First, there are some *huge* tricks and tips I will tell you that will make you stand out at any company, no matter how many people are in line. These tricks have *proven* to be very effective by candidates and vets I have taught across the US from coast to coast. But they are rarely used and I always wondered why for years; until I discovered that veterans just don't know about them.

I'm surprised that many vets are not quite sure what their number one priority is at a job fair. Yes, they want to impress company reps in hopes to get hired....but hold on. That sounds right, but you're missing a big step. Simply put, your number one priority should be *to get an interview*. It is not to get a job. At least not yet. What company would talk to you for three minutes at the job fair booth and then just offer you a job without an interview?

Here is what you should do at a job fair, step by step. You should have plenty of copies of your resume. You should be dressed up in your interview clothes...please understand: to recruiters, the job fair is a mini-interview or a short screening interview. Your job is to impress them enough so that they send you to the next step. For many companies, that is an interview. Now, it could be the next day or it might be a phone interview at some time in the future. But the bottom line is this: your job at a job fair is to impress the recruiter enough so that he will want to send you to the next step in the process, which is usually an interview.

But how do you do that with so many people trying to do the same thing? Well, there are some specific things you can do to greatly enhance your chances. For example, having a past performance evaluation to give to the recruiters behind the booth is *extremely* effective; it needs to be good of course. In the upcoming chapter on Interviewing, one of the key mantras widely accepted in the interview literature is that past performance is a good indicator of future performance. I would agree. That is why they usually ask you questions that are "behavioral" in the interview. Recruiters want to hear about what you have done in the past because it is a gauge of how you will perform in the future. But what does that have to do with the job fair? Well, remember, I said the time in front of the company rep at the booth is a mini interview.

HUGE TIP #1:   Bring Past Performance Evaluations

So now, you show up to the job fair booth. You are dressed properly, and you are prepared. However, so are most of those great candidates in line with you...and not everyone is going to succeed at The Prime Directive (to get an interview) because there is a limited number of interview slots. For example, at the job fair booth, I pick probably one out of every ten to fifteen candidates to interview. But you don't have to worry about that. You have something extra. You have something that will most assuredly show them they should take a chance on you and give you an interview. You have something that will reduce their fear of making the mistake of picking the wrong person. This something is a copy of your past performance evaluation. This is *huge*. What is more powerful than handing them your resume and then handing them a past performance evaluation that is excellent?   There are very few tips or tricks that have this level of effectiveness at changing a recruiter's mind-set over to your side so quickly.

I cannot express to you how powerful this is. Again, as we talked about, recruiting is not an exact science. It's not a hard science like a mathematical equation where it's either a right or wrong answer. Yes, companies have official interview forms that quantifiably score each person on the same set of criteria. But there is no way, I repeat, *no way* to take all the subjectivity out of the equation. As long as you're dealing with human beings, true objectivity is just about impossible. Just think back to the way things work at boot camp. Everybody gets the same haircut, the same uniforms, sleeps in the same rooms, and eats the same meals. In theory, the whole process is absolutely objective...and every recruit is on exactly the same footing. But that absolute equality didn't last

> *Offering a written document from another company, by your past boss illustrating you are a top performer is powerful.*

long, did it?   Before a week was up, you probably could tell whether you were on the drill sergeant's good side or bad side.

In this situation, you are at the job fair. Your job is to impress the recruiter enough to get an interview. By you offering a written document from another company, by your past boss illustrating that you are a top performer is powerful. If your past work performance has been great, to a recruiter that means not only are you well prepared, but you have shown you are willing to take the extra step; go the extra mile. It shows them quickly that you are proud of your past work and your past performance, and you are essentially saying to the recruiter, "This is the kind of performance you can expect if you help me get into your company."

Jackpot!

By providing them a copy of a past performance evaluation, you have shown them you are not just another candidate. You have shown them that the risk they have in choosing you for an interview and potential job is low. You have shown them that you are prepared and have the right attitude. Try it. You have nothing to lose and everything to gain. This just might be that one thing that gets you the interview.

The best performance evaluations are those that are quantifiable; in other words, they score you on a scale of numbers. Also, they need to be signed by your manager or your boss. A letter of recommendation is NOT a performance evaluation and it's not quantifiable. It's not the same thing, nor does it carry even close to the same weight. As a matter of fact, it carries very little weight simply because I know it's going to put you in a positive light. But a performance evaluation scores or ranks you in many performance areas. It just doesn't simply say you were great, it tells the story of your greatness across many categories.

Don't make the mistake of bring multiple copies of many different past performance evaluations. One is enough. My suggestion is to take your most recent performance review and use that. Make multiple copies of that one and hand a copy out each time you hand out your resume at a job fair. The best way to present it is easy, just say something like this, "Here is a copy of my resume along with a copy of my past performance evaluation." It's that easy.

Now, there are exceptions when doing this. Obviously if your most recent performance evaluation is not good, you should find a better one from your past and use that. Now, if all of your past performance reviews are bad, well, don't use them....and there just might be a larger problem you need to address.

As we discussed before, there are a lot of vets with secret or top secret clearance. This means you can't talk about what you did specifically. But having a great past performance evaluation really helps here as well because in that particular case, it is not what you did specifically, but how was your performance at doing whatever you did. Past job performance is what interests most employers. So again, you're giving them what they want to see, quickly. You're speaking their language.

HUGE TIP #2:   Listen For the Questions

You are prepared, you have plenty of copies of your resume and your past performance evaluation, and you are standing in line waiting to talk to the recruiter behind the job fair booth. Why is it that while standing in line most candidates talk to one another, talk on their cell phone, text message, or look around, seemingly in a daze? What if there was a way for you to know the questions we are going to ask you *before* you get up to the booth. Would that be helpful to you? Well there is. Here's how:

While standing in the line of companies that are at the top of your list to work for, listen to the questions that the recruiters are asking the candidates ahead of you. This is simple yet brilliant. Why? Because recruiters for the most part develop a script or set of questions they like to ask all candidates at the job fair. This is human nature. Do you think we make up new questions for everyone we see? Well, we don't. In general, we stick to the same few questions for each candidate. That is why if you listen to the questions we are asking the candidates ahead of you, we will probably ask you the same ones or some of the same ones. In the job fair seminar that I teach to live audiences, I even go as far as telling the students that before they stand in line, to approach the booth casually and to listen to the questions. Then write them down. Next, go to the end of the line and while you are waiting, formulate your answers. If you are not comfortable with that, after you listen to the questions, walk to some quiet corner of the room and formulate your answers. Then, get back in line and practice them until you are next. If you don't like either of those methods, get a friend to do some reconnaissance for you. Have them causally listen in on the questions and report back to you. Now, that I think about it, you could even ask someone that just got done talking to the recruiter, "What questions did they ask you?" This is nothing less than brilliant and will give you a BIG strategic advantage.

Yes, there are times when we see something on your resume that we ask specifically about, but it's usually something positive that we picked up on. Also, at job fair booths that have little traffic, the recruiters have a lot more time to spend so they might ask you more questions…but that is because they have time because they don't have a lot of people coming to their booth. So now you have even less competition, and those tips I have mentioned still are extremely effective.

HUGE TIP #3: Ask for an Interview

This tip is probably the most effective tip I have seen used successfully many, many times but only if you do it the right way. Don't make the mistake of thinking that if you just ask for an interview, you will get one, although you might. **You have to both do it at the right time and use the right words.** This is the key. Here is how: You did both Huge Tip No. 1 and No. 2 and you are talking to the recruiter. Chances are that if you followed those tips the recruiter is just signing you up for an interview. But what if that has not happened yet and the conversation is winding down? Let's say the recruiter starts to say something like, "Well, you have some really good things on your resume. Make sure you go apply online, and you have a good chance at getting noticed." Then, the recruiter reaches out his/her hand to shake yours. What this means is that you didn't get an interview, and they are trying to politely conclude with you and get on to the next person.

But wait. You still have a great opportunity to get an interview. This is when you use one of the most effective tips I teach. I would call it a "Hail Mary" play, but it's much more effective than that. This is exactly what you say, "I would really appreciate an interview with you. If you grant me an interview, I promise I won't let you down." *Powerful.*

Read it again, but read it slow. Do you see the emotion? Do you see that it is not only a personal plea, but a *personal promise* that you're making to the recruiter? This is psychology, and it works.

You have now infused emotion into the equation. You have gotten the recruiter out of their script and out of their comfort zone and you, in two sentences, made it personal. You made yourself the underdog. Everyone loves to root for the underdog. I have seen how effective this tip is because I came up with it and I have taught it. You would not believe how successful this technique is. What do you have to lose? Nothing. You were being told to go to the website. You were done. But then you came *thundering back* with this statement. You changed the game. It works. *Just do it.*

HUGE TIP WORKS: Recently, I was at an event in Florida and I was scheduled to teach two seminars: one "The Secrets of Applying Online" and the other, "How To Negotiate Salary." Well, so many people showed up to each of them that the event manager had to turn people away. Because there was an hour between the different seminars, the event manager approached me and asked if I would give back-to-back seminars. I ended up teaching several hundred people that day at four seminars. In the last seminar, in the question and answer portion, one guy asked me to give him my best tip for getting an interview for a job fair he was attending the next day. I told him and the rest of the audience, the Huge Tip #3 above. The next day, near the end of the job fair, that same guy came up to me at the booth. He introduced himself, and I told him I remembered him from the day before. He told me he just stopped by to thank me. He said the last job fair he went to, he did not get one interview. He then said he used my advice I just gave him the day before. He said he now had several interviews the next day and was very excited. He admitted that he felt a little stressed because he had so many and was anxious to get home to prepare. Finally, he said he felt he should stop by and let me know the success he had by following my advice, even though my company didn't have the job he wanted. Then he thanked me again and left. This kind of situation happens every time I teach a seminar before the job fair. He was the fourth person that day to come up to the booth and thank me for the advice. Each had great success, and so will you if you just try it.

Look, the chance of you *not* scoring an interview if you follow the **3 HUGE TIPS** is slim. I'm not giving you 20 tips to follow. I'm simply giving you the *top three* that I know work most of the time for vets. Even if you just use one of these tips, your chances of getting an interview greatly increase because you made yourself stand out and set yourself apart. You did something that most candidates at the job fair just do not do. In a sea of candidate at a job fair, vets that use these 3 HUGE TIPS will stand out in a positive way and those are the people that get interviews.

Now, you might ask me:

- Do I approach small, medium, and large companies the same?

- Don't I change my approach significantly when I'm talking with a small company as opposed to the large company?

- Having the same approach for different sized companies can't possibly work, can it?

I hear questions like this all the time. In my career as a recruiter, I have been involved in the recruiting process for small, medium and large companies. Why is it that candidates feel as if there is something they need to change in their approach just because of the size of a company? For the most part, the approach is exactly the same. Your job is to put your best foot forward. Stand out in a positive way. Be prepared and

> *Whether you are trying to acquire a job at a small, medium, or large company your approach basically stays the same.*

follow up. Why would a recruiter from a small, medium, or large company be looking for anything different? Now, maybe they're looking for different skills, but if you think about it, *all* recruiters want the best candidates they can find. So why change your approach?

Yes there are small differences. For example, at job fairs, some of the big companies have three booth spaces and a dozen recruiters. They have huge lines that sometimes you are waiting in for thirty minutes or more. On the other hand, I have seen small and even medium-sized companies have no lines and just one booth with just one or two company representatives. If you are approaching those booths, obviously, you can't listen for the question they are asking someone in front of you in line, when there is no line. Moreover, since there is a short or no line at all, the recruiters will have the luxury of spending more time with you; asking you more questions and talking with you more. However, this gives you a great chance to stand out because you have even less competition. But all recruiters look for the same things. They look for the best candidates, no matter what size the company is.

That being said, in general, the smaller the company the more time they have to evaluate each candidate, and the more time they take reading each candidate's resume. I remember when I was involved with recruiting for a small company; I would read everything only because there were not a lot of applicants. I read every line of the resume and even read the cover letter. But when recruiting for a big company, I have many, many more people to consider. I had to change my process to more of a scanning of the resume only, at least initially. Either way, you win because you are prepared more than every other candidate. If it's a big company, they have more candidates to look at and less time to spend with each one. They will most likely give interviews to the ones that quickly impress them. In smaller companies, they will normally have fewer candidates to pick from and will spend a little more time with each candidate. They will pick those candidates that impress them the most. Whichever is the case, you will be one of those candidates if you follow the upcoming advice.

Another thing to remember when you are at a job fair or any career related events, be happy to be there. Too many vets and other candidates I see seem to be worn down by the process of finding a job. I know it's not always fun. I know if you have been looking for a job for a while you may feel a little desperate or even down about not having a job. I completely understand. But those people behind the job fair booth want to recommend people that are happy and friendly; people that are enthusiastic about their company and about talking to them about their company. Those behind the booth want to recommend vets with a great "can do" attitude. So I understand that sometimes it's not easy to put on a happy face at these events and be "up" for them. But what you will find is that if you approach the job fair and do the 3 HUGE TIPS, you will most likely see a positive response. Once that happens, it's easy for you to feel better about being there and trying. I understand how nerve racking these events can be for some veterans.   But now you have some *really powerful tools* and if you use them every time all the time, you will get results.

Lastly, if you happen to get any business cards or contacts from the job fair, follow up with them via email with a copy of your resume and a copy of your past performance evaluation within twenty-four hours and *thank* them for the time they spent with you. Follow up is another key critical skill employers are

> *There's a ridiculous amount of information out there on interviewing. Here's what works* **BEST…and** *all that* **you really need to** *know.*

looking for. You should go into a job fair understanding there are two main events. The first is the job fair itself. The second is your follow up after the job fair. This is *very* important and oftentimes, it's the difference in making the decision to interview a candidate. Remember, interviews don't necessarily happen right after the job fair. Some recruiters and company hiring managers what to review those they met and then decide. Following up quickly will help them remember you and remember that you were a candidate that went the extra mile.

Chapter 5

Interviews

One easy-to-remember method, 3 Fantastic Tips, and the most effective way to follow up.

How do you know that you did badly in an interview? What if you are making the same mistake in every interview with every company, and that mistake is preventing you from getting an offer? The only way you will know this is if you go to a professional career counselor, do mock interviews and get feedback. That way, the professional counselors will be able to spot it and help you correct it. But it still doesn't answer the question, "So what does it really take to be a great interviewee; to really impress an interviewer?"

Again, nearly 15 years of interviewing thousands of candidate leads me to what you will learn in this section. There are many elements. We can discuss body language, how to dress, what to do if you have sweaty palms, basically, all these topics you find in many of the other "How-To" interview books that are a billion pages long. Many of those topics are helpful. But can I just assume that you know these things or will find out how to address them before you interview so we can get down to business? For example, the subject of dressing appropriately. After all, your choice of tie or color of pantsuit is really low on the totem pole when it comes to scoring huge in an interview. Yes, yes....you need to dress correctly, conservatively. That means guys, have a suit and tie (a boring tie...you know, the kind your grandfather would wear, or the kind you would wear to a funeral...not a Mickey Mouse or Hooters' tie).

Gals, wear a nice boring pantsuit. Go into your closet and get the most boring outfit you have and wear that.

Dressing correctly is *not* going to get you the job; but dressing like an idiot can definitely blow your chances of getting it, so stick with this advice. You need to show the interviewer that you can "play ball" which means you understand that in the interview environment you need to fit in when it comes to dress….not stand out. For example, you and I don't know what biases the interviewer may have. Remember, your goal is to do everything you can to show them you are great, you will fit in, and you won't be a problem. Be polite, be professional, dress appropriately, and fit in. Again, the number one fear of hiring managers and recruiters is hiring someone who is a problem. So, if you start off the interview dressed inappropriately, do you see how that can translate into the interviewer being less inclined to recommend you? It throws up a red flag right away and puts you in a potential uphill battle. Plus, it is a first impression. You need to ensure it is a good one or you may not ever recover.

> *Interviewing is nothing more than telling stories. You are essentially scored on how well you tell stories about you and your experiences.*

REMEMBER YOUR SOCKS: One late October, early in my career, I was in upstate New York, and I was doing fall recruiting for my company. Now, for those of you familiar with upstate New York in late October…it can be beautiful. But it can also be cold and snowy, and there were about two inches of snow on the ground. At around noon, I went to lunch in the cafeteria. After I sat down, my mentor, Dr. Campbell (the lead recruiter and a Ph.D. in chemical engineering) approached me with someone I didn't recognize. His suit was wrinkled, his hair didn't look as if it had been combed, and his tie was loosened up so that the tie knot was about three inches down from where it should be. They both came over and sat down with me. My immediate evaluation of the situation was that Dr. Campbell was being followed around by a candidate that was trying to impress him and talking about anything and everything he could think of. (Sometimes that happens to recruiters). I then noticed that this guy wasn't even wearing socks. With two inches of snow on the ground, he took the time to wear a suit but had no socks. *Not a good first impression.* Dr. Campbell introduced me to him as Dave Johnson, and I shook his hand and said hello, but I stayed out of the conversation since I was eating. Afterwards, Dave got up and left.

Not five minutes went by, and Dr. Campbell asked me what I thought of the guy. I told him that I was not very impressed, and why. Then, believe it or not, he asked me to put him on my interview schedule. I looked up at him with what I'm sure was confusion on my face, and said, "Why?" He then answered, "Let's see what he can do."

The next day, Dave showed up to his interview. Same suit; same wrinkles…and still no socks. I thought to myself, "What a waste of my time," and was less than enthusiastic about interviewing him. *I mean, come on, no socks with a suit, with snow on the ground?* Looking back on it, I was inexperienced, and basically, I had my mind made up that this guy was not the caliber of candidate my company was looking for. But then I started the interview. I asked him the same questions as all the other candidates. I remember being surprised when he really answered the first question well—really well. Then he answered the second and third questions equally well. It took me over half the interview to even start warming up to how good his answers were…all because he wore no socks.

Now, this might seem odd or even unfair to you: I was essentially pre-judging someone because of what he wore, or in this case *didn't* wear, to the interview. But do you think that is professional, him not having any socks on for the interview? Remember, one of my jobs as a recruiter is to evaluate him on whether or not he would be the right fit for my company. But Dave was exceptional. He was brilliant and yet very personable. His answers to my questions were outstanding. He knew how to answer questions in the correct format and time (which I will teach later in this book). So, at the end of the interview, I had to make a choice: recommend him, no socks and all, or not recommend him.

And this is the point: why would I even consider not recommending him if he was that good? The point of the story is to illustrate the importance of dressing correctly. Yes, Dave overcame it because he was truly exceptional. But most of us are not, so why put ourselves into an uphill battle? Plus, do not make the assumption that those interviewing you will overlook things like the absence of socks. Most won't.

I did highly recommend Dave, and he did get hired with my company. If I remember correctly, I actually hired him in. I also remember taking great pleasure making fun of him whenever I could work the "no socks" story in with the other interns. After he was with my company for a while, he left and accepted a position with another company that gave him a job he always wanted to try (my company just didn't have that same type of job). This was a huge talent loss for my company, but this is part of being a recruiter sometimes.

You might know Dave: he was on one season of *Survivor* and was known as the Rocket Scientist—he really *is* a rocket scientist. I just reconnected with him again when I saw him at a recent career fair at Massachusetts Institute of Technology (MIT). He left his position at the company he was working for and had gone back to school for a Master's degree and was interested in investigating fulltime opportunities with my company. I will definitely do whatever I can to help him get in. It is rare to find a candidate that is as good as Dave is in so many areas. And yes, he was wearing socks this time.

So, how do you prepare yourself for interviews? Can't there just be one simple way that will let you learn how to answer most if not all interview questions really well without having to memorize a bunch of stories that some book told you on how to answer questions like, "What is your greatest weakness?"

There is a way. It works. I know it works because for nearly 15 years, many, many candidates have e-mailed me thanking me for teaching them this method. But I have boiled it down to just a few key factors. What you are really looking for is a method to help you become a great interviewee. I have taken some of what is already out there and refined it to create one focused approach for vets. This approach makes it easy for vets to take their military experience and transform it into a format that civilian employers love!

GETTING TO THE POINT

Most first interviews are now Behavior Interviews or sometimes called "Structural Interviews." This is commonplace now. You want to know why? Because those making the hiring decisions generally believe that past behavior and performance are great indicators of future behavior and performance; a lot of the literature supports this view. So the belief is, when you are interviewing with a company, your behavior on past assignments and at past jobs is the strongest indicator of what you will do for them. So you must have specific examples, and they must be in the form of a story. They must be direct, succinct, organized, and structured.

Recruiters try to keep emotion out of the process of recruiting, and you really are trying to keep it in. You want to answer the questions so well, so smoothly, that the interviewer will want to take it personal whether or not you get into the company. You want the person that interviews you to "champion" you. If your interview answers are so good, they will take "championing" you personally. This is your goal.

Interviewing is nothing more than telling stories. You are essentially scored on how well you tell stories about you and your experiences. So, why is it so hard and stressful for some? Some say because it is like a test. You really never know what they are going to ask. Plus, you are talking to a complete stranger and in a small time, trying to stand out, impress, and convince them that you are "all that and a bag of chips." This is nerve-racking for most vets. I know it was for me when I was in your spot, but there is a solution.

There are many methods out there: STAR (Situation, Task, Action, Result), SBO (Situation, Behavior, and Outcome), SAO (Situation, Action, and Outcome), SAR (Situation, Action, and Result), and others. I don't really care which one you use, but use one of them because they are all leading you down the same correct path. I prefer SBO because the "B" stands for Behavior and that is really what is being tested in a behavioral interview. The "B" is a good reminder for you to focus on your behavior and that each question is trying to evaluate you on your past behavior.

The key to all of these methods is to prepare and to have examples in the form of a story. Any question they ask should be answered detailing: **S, B, O, and should be completed in about 90 seconds.** That leaves you approximately 30 seconds for Situation, 30 seconds for Behavior, and 30 seconds for Outcome. I would say allow yourself 10 seconds total either way but no more and no less. In other words, your entire answer should lie between 80 – 100 seconds with the sweet spot at 90 seconds. If it is much shorter than this, usually there is not enough detail in your answer to warrant a really high score. If it is much longer than this, there is usually too much detail or it is not organized enough for the interviewer to quickly see what they need to. Although each section (S, B, O) is very important and a must have to score high, if I had to choose which one was most important, I would have to pick Behavior. This is because all recruiters, interviewers, and hiring managers should know what I have told you already and that is *past behavior is the best indicator of future behavior.*

Here is how you get started: You should have 6 or more stories ready to go. Focus your stories on areas or topics that companies most likely will ask. Here are some:

- Leadership
- Dealing with a difficult person
- Adaptability
- Helping others (without being told to do so)
- What did you do when something went wrong?
- Solving a Problem
- Your Greatest Strength
- Your Greatest Weakness
- Your Greatest Accomplishment
- Your Greatest Disappointment

Now, I know what you are saying: "I thought we weren't supposed to memorize answers and regurgitate them back." This is different. These are stories about your life—your experiences. You already know them because you lived them. So really all you have to do is to tell your stories back to the interviewer in the S, B, O format. That's it. You don't have to memorize them because they are your experiences; you already know them.

What I suggest is to take a piece of paper and write down each of the topic areas above. Then put S, B, O below them and start filling in your story. Concentrate on the Situation first. Then move to Behavior, YOUR behavior. Finally, work on the Outcome. Once you have that down, all you really need to do is make sure the timing and details are in each section and you got it. Yes, you will have to practice them so they flow. Yes, it will take you an hour or two to develop and practice your stories, but that is all. Plus, you spent at least that much time on your resume, so if you just spend the same amount of time rehearsing your stories, you will do great. This is a critical step if you want success. Remember, companies hire the person, not the resume.

So you want more help developing the SBO, well I'm here for you. Below are the important aspects of S, B, and O.

SITUATION (S): The Situation section is where you illustrate to the interviewer in words the environment that you are in and perhaps how you got there. You explain the scene. Your job is to paint a picture of where you are, what you are doing, what you are responsible for, the problem you need to solve, etc. **Use details.** Describe your surroundings. Describe the assignment you were given. Describe things like how many people you were on your team and what was your goal or objective. Do all this in 30 seconds. If you are doing it in less than 30 seconds, most likely you need to add more details. If it is more than 30 seconds, you need to cut out some of the details and become more succinct and more organized about telling the situation.

BEHAVIOR (B): This is where you describe YOUR behavior. Not what the team did but what *you* did specifically. **This is the key section because this is what they are looking for most.** If it is the first question, the interviewer is looking for a good example of you using good judgment, good initiative, good problem solving skills, etc. Then, if you do well on that first question, on the rest of the questions they will be looking for a trend or consistency in your behavior. A tip here: If you or your friends that you practice your stories with think your behavior is what most people would do in a similar situation, then this is a good indicator that your story is probably good at best. You want *great.* If your behavior, as you explain it, is above and beyond what most people will do in a similar situation, now you have an excellent chance at scoring great. Great candidates often go the extra mile and do one more thing than most people would do in a similar situation. Remember, details are the key. You want to tell the interviewer what your specific behaviors were (what your plan was, how you approached coming up with that plan, how you implemented that plan). Then you want to explain how your specific behaviors led to the success or your achievement of the goal.

OUTCOME (O): A first piece of advice here: you might want to make the outcome *positive.* I have seen 100 times how someone does well in painting a great picture in the Situation. Then, in the Behavior section goes above and beyond what the normal person would do and explains the specifics of what they did. Then, in the Outcome section describes that the project or task they were responsible for failed, but they say they learned a lot. Talk about torpedoing the ship. Come on. If the outcome of a story is not positive, then get another story. The danger in the Outcome section always seems to be the length. Remember, like the first two sections, it needs to be 30 seconds. Too many people forget this and when they get to the Outcome section, they simply say, "It was successful," or "The goal was met." You can't do that. Yes you should say the Outcome was a success but you should explain WHY it was a success. Or explain how you know it was a success. For example: Did your commander comment that the job was well done? If so what exactly did he/she say? Details. Another way to look at explaining the Outcome is you trying to PROVE it was successful. You present the EVIDENCE as to why it was successful and how you know it was successful.

> *If the Outcome [O] of your story is not positive, get another story!*

Now, the next step is to assist you with questions I always seem to get like, "But how do I answer questions like, "What is your greatest strength?" and "What is your greatest weakness?" These are what I like to refer to as "critical questions." That means, that it is critical for you to do well on these questions, even if it is only well enough to get through the question and on to the next one without any trouble.

You see, recruiters like to peer into your soul if they can. Critical questions seem to help us do that quickly because they make you almost instantly prioritize significant things about yourself and about your life. They make you pick one thing, one event, one example from all your life experiences to answer one question. That is powerful because it gives the interviewer a window into who you are. What you believe. What is important to you. What you are about. Yes, I know, it is only one question. But over an entire interview, those critical questions, and others, often act as a roadmap to who you are and what you will be like as an employee. Sometimes, it may give an interviewer just a glimpse of an area that they want to probe further or get clarification on. Remember, this is not an exact science. Yes, good and great interviewers try hard to just score you based on a set of criteria and nothing else. But there are always times when something just doesn't sound right, or when the answer to the question, perhaps because of the words that the candidate uses, seems to indicate that there is more there. Trained interviewers will probe those areas to make sure they have the whole picture, the whole story. In the end, critical questions are no different than any other question when it comes down to what you need to do to answer them. Just follow the same S, B, O approach above, and you will do great.

FANTASTIC TIP #1:
Your story is about what *you* did, *not* what the team did.

Don't make the mistake of answering interview questions with what the team did. I want to know what YOU did. I'm not interviewing the team. I know, I know, you want me to see that you're a "team player" and can work as a part of a team. I get it. Corporate America has stressed the importance of working as a part of a team, of being a team player. But I'm not interviewing the team. I'm interviewing you. As a vet or person in the military, you should already have a large number of stories about times you functioned as part of a team. When you tell them, make sure to focus on what YOU did within that team.

FANTASTIC TIP #2:
Ask for the job.

No one ever just asks for the job and that is a tragedy because it often works. This may be the difference between you getting the job and someone else getting it. Asking for the job gives you an edge and makes it crystal clear that you are interested and committed. You do it at the very end, just as you are about to leave. This is what you say: "There is one last thing I would like to ask you. I would like to ask you for the job. It sounds exciting and is just what I'm looking for. I promise I will work hard for you." Come on. Is there any question the interviewer(s) will remember you now? Look, suppose you are a little shy or a little nervous in the interview; or a lot nervous. Some of your enthusiasm about the position might be stifled because of this. You never want to leave the interviewer wondering if you really want the job. If you do, that is a sure-fire way for them to choose someone else. With the four short sentences above there will be no question in the interviewer's mind that you want the position. You will stand out. They will remember you.

You have a better chance at getting the job if you just ask for it. Do this at the very end of every interview.

FANTASTIC TIP #3:
Bring a "cheat sheet" to the interview

Did you know that if you are playing blackjack in Las Vegas, you can actually have with you, in plain sight, a card that tells you how to play each hand? This is totally legal, and often the casinos themselves sell these cards in their gift shops. So why don't you do the same thing in your interviews? Why don't you just bring some notes with you that remind you what your stories are? This is totally acceptable, yet few people do it. Many vets worry they won't remember all their stories under pressure. This is understandable. I know many people just get really nervous and have this fear that they might "lock up". Chances are, if you prepared, you will do great and won't even need your notes, but having them there as a reminder may help. Also, in your notes, why not write S, B, O to remind yourself that on every answer, these three things need to be in your answer.

"But what if they ask me a question that doesn't fit with any of the stories I came up with?" I get asked this question from time to time. The answer is that you will find most of your stories flexible enough to answer many different questions. That is the beauty of this approach. You will discover that the answer for your greatest strength might also be a great answer for your greatest accomplishment or even dealing with a difficult person.

However, if you find yourself in that situation, and none of your stories seem to fit, the great thing is that you already know what you need to do. You have practiced how to answer any interview question with Situation, Behavior, and Outcome. In the interview, bring a piece of paper, and if a question comes up like that, simply write down "S,B,O," to remind yourself and think about an experience you had that would answer the question. Simply start off with the situation, then move on to behavior, and, finally, the outcome. Believe me, at the very least, you will do a lot better than most.

Another question candidates always ask me is, "But what if they give me one of those overly general questions?" Ok, suppose you are asked, "Tell me a little about yourself." Why does everyone panic on this question? This is GREAT. You are hoping for this question. You know why? Because it is your chance to break out your best story and tell it. All you really need to do is have a good transition or lead in like, "I think the best way to get to know me is to know what my greatest strength is. Let me give you an example."   Then you just break into that story.

WHAT *YOU* SHOULD ASK IN THE INTERVIEW

There is another thing you should have in the notes you prepare and bring with you to the interview—questions. Write down the questions that you should ask the interviewer. Notice how I didn't say the questions you *want* to ask. There is a difference. Ask only three questions, and then ask for the job.

You are at the end of the interview process, and the interviewer is asking you if you have any questions. This is the perfect opportunity to finish strong so you should phrase your first question in a way that tries to impress the interviewer one last time.

Your first question should start with a statement of specific fact about the company, followed by a question relating to that fact. For example, "I noticed you recently acquired XYZ Company into your research and development group. How will that increase your market share globally?" The strategy here is so start off with a statement that shows you did your homework about the company. The statement part of the question shows you took the initiative to research the company, that you went the extra mile. Asking the question was not really about getting the answer to the question. It was about giving them one more example, right at the end of the interview, of what they can expect if they hire you. They may not know the answer, and you don't really care. Your job was to show them, one last time, that you were both prepared and researched the company. This should be your first question.

The second question should verify the interviewer's contact information to follow up with them after the interview. I would get their name, e-mail address, mailing address, and phone number if you can. This is critical for you to show them how great you are with following up on the interview. Getting this information gives you a chance to show them you will go the extra mile one last time as well as reminding them who you are.

The third and last question you ask, *before* you ask for the job of course, should always be about the interviewer. *Always.* Why?

Because you want to get the interviewer talking about him or herself. When people have a chance to talk about themselves, about their career or their accomplishments, it makes them feel good. Remember, this is one of the last things you before you leave and they score you so leaving them shortly after

> *The very last thing you do before you walk out is to ask for the job.*

they got to talk about themselves and they are feeling good, well it helps. And guess what? Many times your scores go up. Some of you might not believe this can happen, but it does all the time. People like other people who are interested in hearing their story. Please don't under estimate what I call the "likability factor" which is people hire who they like. When scoring you after you leave, interviewers are not immune from this, and although no one can guarantee that it will raise your scores, give it a try. You have nothing to lose and everything to gain.

Then of course, the very last thing you do before you walk out is *ask for the job.*

FOLLOWING UP AFTER THE INTERVIEW

Every book I have read about interviewing tells you to follow up. I am telling you that as well. It is very important. It is often the deciding factor if it is a close decision between candidates. However, many people feel that e-mailing the interviewers to thank them is the best way. It is becoming more and more accepted as the standard thing to do; so you should do it. But the best way to follow up is old school. It is a hand- written thank you note. In the note, you should thank them, of course, but also include one fact from the interview, one specific positive point.

The reason you do this is to help them remember you and keep them remembering you. The last thing you should do in the thank you note is again to ask for the job. So many times, this step is left out; however, I think it is an effective way of conveying to them that you are serious about their company and want the job. Yes, the assumption is if you are going through all these steps, of course, you want the job. But there were many times in my career, especially when it was a close race between one or more candidates, when a candidate asked for the job and that impressed someone enough to bring it up in the debate or argument for them. Plus, often that person got chosen.

There are different methods on how to send the thank you note. Regular mail is normally too slow...but it has its place. For example, if you immediately (which means within 12 hours of the interview) e-mail them off a thank you e-mail, you can also follow up with a thank you card by mail. This lets a few days go by between your e-mail and when they get the hand written thank you card. This is good because it reminds them of you again and shows that you went one extra step and are willing to go the extra mile. This is powerful.

> *Even in this day and age of e-mail, hand written "thank you" notes are still very effective and should be part of your follow up process.*

Now, you can also send a hand-written note FedEx or UPS overnight.

Again, that shows the extra step, and it will normally get their attention. But the expense is pretty high. Plus, this adds up fast if you have interviewed with several companies.

But I have a solution. After sending the normal thank you e-mail, try this: It is my favorite way of sending a thank you note and what I believe is the most effective hands down. Send the thank you note Priority Mail, but send it in a Priority Mail TUBE. Yes, a *tube*. Now, I expect you have a smile on your face right now. But when was the last time someone sent you something in a tube? We all get things next-day air, at least from time to time. But when was the last time anyone sent you anything in a tube? When employers get a tube, they immediately are curious. They want to open the tube and see what's in it...because *no one ever gets a tube*. Someone could have a hundred other pieces of mail, and I bet you, the first one that gets opened is the tube. It is inexpensive, original, and different. It will get and keep their attention. It will make you stand out. Plus, it shows you are creative and willing to again, go the extra mile and take one more step than most candidates would take. It may sound silly, but it really works. Try it.

question, and so on. There is nothing more complicated about it. In addition, there is nothing different you would do in a panel interview than you would in a one-on-one interview except direct your answers to the person asking the question. If anything else, if you follow my advice, you'll just impress more people, so don't worry about panel interviews and just stick to what you have learned.

Chapter 6

How to Negotiate Salary

Learn in only 3 STEPS exactly how to do it, including a technique that will maximize your chances at getting more money.

Negotiation is said to be an art form. There are entire books dedicated to negotiating one thing or another including your pay. From my experience most people including vets are not comfortable with it. Plus those negotiating with you for the company, well they do it all the time so they have the upper hand; at least they did before now.

There are too many vets that are just uncomfortable negotiating their salary simply for the fact that they don't know how or they don't know the best way to do it. Some don't even try to negotiate at all. I'm hoping to change that because without even trying to negotiate your salary, you are selling yourself short and leaving a lot of money on the table.

Many years ago, my brother-in-law recommended a book to me titled *Knock'em Dead,* by Martin Yate. It is especially good when you have a number of years of experience under your belt. I believe it is still one of the best books out there for preparing experienced people for the job search. I especially like the chapter on salary negotiation. I know some of Yate's suggestions helped me at different times along my career, and that is why you may see some similarities. What I have tried to do is take what I have learned over the years, along with some of his suggestions that have helped me, and come up with a simple method of negotiating salary.

Did you know that failing to negotiate your salary, even by a few thousand, could cost you $200,000 or so over a career? That is called, "Time Value of Money," and if you're an MBA, you know exactly what I'm talking about. That's an awfully large amount of money to leave on the table. So, if there is one point I want to make in this chapter, it is to TRY.

Again, those people who fail to negotiate are just very uncomfortable with the process. Some think if they do, they'll blow it, and the company will take back the offer, leaving them with nothing. Others are concerned that they will sound too greedy. Still others are scared that it won't work, and they will fail.

Negotiating salary is really not that complex. It really boils down to two things (1.) being realistic about the range of salary in your field (2.) Asking for it in a way that is courteous, respectful, and yet very effective.

STEP #1: Get The Data

Learning how to negotiate your salary is all about data, research, and preparation. It is about you taking some time to investigate what I like to call the Salary Market Range (SMR). The SMR is nothing more than getting on the Internet and finding out what salary range is appropriate for your level of experience in the job that you are getting an offer for. You are interested in the low and high salary range. This is the base information you need.

The bottom line here is that you have to define for yourself a low and high number for your salary range. The difference between these numbers needs to be realistic; I would say about five to six thousand dollars. To get to several good sources for you, your experience level and your career there are many good tools out there. Each tool has their strengths and weaknesses but the easiest way to find your range is simply to Google "What salary should I ask for" and spend a little time surfing a few sites. In a very short period of time you will have a good workable salary range.

STEP #2: Make a One Page Report

Put together a one-page report. In the report you should have the data you found from your research that supports the salary range you are asking for. (Title it "Executive Briefing: Salary Market Range for [enter your name].") Organize the data in a way that is direct and to the point.

Site those websites and sources where you got your information. Include any charts or graphs that help your cause. No more than one page. Then, at the bottom, the last statement should be: "Conclusion: Appropriate salary range $74,000-$79,000."

I know many of you will not take the time to do this step. Again, I'm realistic when I teach and from my experience some will take the time to do it and some will not. But the importance of this step is twofold. First, by going through this process, it teaches and confirms what salary range is realistic and appropriate for you. This provides the extra confidence some may need to believe that they are worth what they are asking for, and it will motivate them to actually ask when they normally would not have. Second, it gives you a document you can refer to, e-mail, or fax over to the person you're negotiating with to help motivate them to increase your salary. Even if they have other data that might dispute yours, even if they don't agree with your data, that is not the point. The point of you sending it over to them is to show them you did your homework, that you are prepared, that you are taking this seriously, and that you're willing to go the extra mile. But, above all, it

> *Google the phrase: "What salary should I ask for" to start your research on what your market value is and what your salary range should be.*

shows them that they will be getting an employee with all these great attributes if they just come up a little on the salary range. *Ding! Ding! Ding! Ding!* That's the sound of more money.

Once you have your range and your Executive Briefing, now you are ready to go to the next step, which is how to ask for more money. I'm going to give you a simple and effective way that you can remember even under pressure. From my experience and as I previously stated, I know many vets are just uncomfortable with this process. Some so uncomfortable that you just won't do it. Others are so nervous or just stressed out over this; again, they won't even attempt it. Even if you're not too stressed, you need a good technique and method that will work for anyone you are negotiating with. In reality, it is not always your direct manager or even anyone in your chain of command that you may be negotiating with. But you are not in control of who you will be negotiating with, so you need one way that will work most of the time with most people. It needs to be simple and not complicated so under pressure you don't forget. Similar to my philosophy on interviewing, you need a process or method that will help you even if the person negotiating with you is not a good negotiator.

STEP #3: Ask For The Money This Way

The first thing you do when getting an offer is to say "Thank You." The key is to be nice, be gracious, and respectful no matter what; even if the one you're negotiating with is not. You never know who is having a bad day. You never know the motivations of the other person.

NEGOTIATION IRRITATION: I have seen people negotiate with potential candidates who just sound irritated and angry when someone tries to negotiate their salary. Later I learned that irritation came from their personal frustration about what they get paid relative to what someone is being offered. I have heard things like, "I have been in the company for ten years, and I don't even make that much," or, "It is not right for this person to make more than me to begin with, and then they ask for more."

For the most part, those that negotiate with you are professionals. But those are not the ones you have to worry about. This is why being nice, respectful, and non-confrontational is so important. You never know who you are going to be negotiating with, and you never know their personal feelings or motivations. I give you this example again to educate you to prepare for the most difficult situation and, therefore, you will be prepared for any situation. In the end, if you follow what is taught in this chapter, it doesn't matter who you are negotiating with. The chances of you getting more money are good.

Negotiating is a lot of psychology, and I could give you all the in-depth psychological reasons why something works, but you might fall asleep so just remember this: The language you use needs to be nice, never confrontational, and never even approaching an ultimatum. Calm, cool, and collected at all times. And always start out by saying, "Thank you for the offer," no matter what the offer is. The reason you do this is to put them in a positive mind set.

Since you have your low and high numbers that make up your range and these numbers are backed up by research and data, you now know what to ask for. Now, if the company representative comes up with a number first, then simply state your range—never just a number.

To give you an example: let's say that after you did your research, your range is $74,000 to $79,000.

They offer you $71,000.

Counter this way: "First, thank you for the offer. We are close. My ideal salary for this position is $79,000 with my range being between $74,000 and $79,000."

That's it. That is all you have to do, at least initially. This will often motivate them to bump you up, and at the very least, put you in a position to be considered for more.

What if they want you to come up with a number first?

Well, this is simple. Since you did the research, you just state the same thing: "First, thank you for the offer. My ideal salary for this position is $79,000, with my range being between $74,000 and $79,000."

What if they give you an offer that is really low, but you really want to work for that company in that job? For example, let's say your range is the same as above, and they offer you $55,000. What then?

Really, nothing changes here. This could be some sort of tactic on the company's part, a method they use to start low in hopes to get you for less money…because again, they know that most prospective employees don't negotiate. Don't worry about that. You just say the same thing: "First, thank you for the offer. We are close. My ideal salary for this position is seventy-nine thousand with my range being between seventy four-and seventy-nine thousand."

Yes, I know they are not close. So why say, "We are close?" Tell them that to keep them in a positive mindset—to keep them on your side.

Now, what if they offer you more than your salary range? That is great!

And you know what you should do? Ask for more. How you do that is what I like to refer to as the Two-Five Rule. Let's continue on with our example range from above $74,000-$79,000. They give you an offer of $81,000 before you even get a chance to state your range. Well, you add $2,000 on to the $81,000 (which makes your bottom range at $83,000), and then add $5,000 on to that (which makes the upper end of your range $88,000). Yes, this is a little simple math. But under stress, I have seen people with master's degrees in engineering unable to do the math on the spot under pressure. That is why I have made it simple. The Two-Five rule. Again, if the initial offer comes in over your range, just add $2,000 on to their offer, and that is your low range number. Then add $5,000 on to that and that is your upper range number. Then you say, "First, thank you for the offer. We are close. My ideal salary for this position is $88,000, with my range being between $83,000 and $88,000 thousand."

See? It's just that easy. Now, I realize that if the initial offer is higher than your range to begin with, then the Executive Briefing you created won't work in its present format and you can just forget about it. But isn't that a nice position to be in?

COMMON QUESTIONS ABOUT SALARY TALKS

There are dozens and dozens of questions I'm asked after presenting this information. The reason is most candidates want the answers to any and all situations that could come up. I can't answer them all, but let me answer a few that come up on a regular basis.

Question: What if after doing everything you said, they just say no?

Answer: Rarely does this actually happen but it does happen. Usually, they say something like, "This is what we start off all people at your level." What you should do in this case is take them off the subject. Ask about benefits. Ask about the corporate culture. Ask about the surrounding area. Ask about what else is included in the offer. Then, after they talk about that for a while, say, "This sounds like a great opportunity and thank you for explaining the details to me. We are close. If we just could move a little on the salary range. My ideal salary for this position is $79,000, with my range being between $74,000 and $79,000 thousand." That sometimes works.

Question: What if they still don't come up?

Answer: Then you have a decision to make. If you really like the job and really like the company, and are ok with the salary, take the position. Some companies just can't or won't give you more money. However, your job was to ask in a way that gave you the best chance at getting more. You did that.

Question: What about in bad economic times? Does your approach change?

Answer: No, not really. If a company is hiring, even in bad economic times, they still want the best person for the job. You should still ask the same way but understand that they may be a little less flexible because they have a lot more candidates to pick from.

Question: What about cost of living?

Answer: Before you get into this argument, you must first evaluate the offer as a whole. For example, companies are aware of the cost of living in different areas. They have to be because if their offers are too low in one part of the country, no one will come to work for them there. But what if a company is willing to pay 100% of your master's degree, but their offer is $10,000 less than another company that will give you nothing towards your education? Well, a good graduate school can be upwards of $20,000 per year. So who really has the better offer? Or look at the benefits package. What if a company gives you $5,000 less a year, but you have excellent medical and dental coverage for both you and your family? And what if the other company is offering only major medical coverage for you the employee and all the other expenses come out of your pocket? The point I'm making is be smart enough to not just jump at the money. Take a look at the value of the whole offer. What you will normally find is that the company that you really want to work for might have a lower offer, but it still might be the best offer.

GOT MORE MONEY: Back when I first came out of college, I scored an interview with a company for a coveted rotational program. It was extremely competitive, and I was told later that out of the best candidates they could find at 136 schools, they only selected eleven for interviews and took the top six for the job. I was lucky enough to be chosen as one of those six.

When my offer came to me, I felt good that I got it, but I was a little let down over the salary. The offer as a whole was an excellent one, but I still wanted to try to see if I could get a little more money. Like most people, I really didn't know how to go about it. I did, however, do the research to find information that would support my asking for more money and put a report together.

Knowing what I know now, I can see that I did a lot of things wrong in the negotiations that followed. However, I did ask for more money, and I did have back-up data. And you know what? *They gave more.* In fact, in their eyes at least, it was a *lot* more, though I didn't know at the time. I didn't figure this out until I arrived for my first day. I remember going into the HR department with a few of the other candidates that had hired in. The HR person did her thing with us: filling out paper work and then entering it into the computer. I was excited. However, when the person got to me, she started to enter all the information, and then had to stop and call a supervisor over. They started to discuss something and then both got irritated. While one of them was doing something on another computer, I was enthusiastically asking a few questions. But the tone and attitude of the HR person had changed. She seemed irritated with me and gave me very short answers. I later found out that because I had negotiated so well, they had to go into their system and override some things to get my salary up to what I was offered. They were not happy because it made more work for them. But I was.

The most important thing about negotiating salary is to *try.* You will probably be surprised by the success you will have and how easy it was getting that success if you follow what you have just learned.

Chapter 7

Cover Letters

The best way to write a cover letter, and why it can give you the edge.

Cover letters are still used, but much less frequently with the advent of the online application process. There seems to be a relationship between the size of the company and the importance of the cover letter. In general the smaller the company, the more important the cover letter is. My theory behind that is that smaller companies have significantly fewer people applying to them so they read everything. And since small businesses hire a lot of vets and if you are planning on doing a cover letter, you will learn in this chapter the best and most effective way to do it.

I want to caution you here. I personally think that cover letters are on their way out, mostly because of the technology they are using to screen candidates. It seems as time goes on cover letters are used less and less frequently. The main document people judge you on is your resume and how well it matches the job they have available. As I stated in the second chapter, if you're applying online, it takes about 40 to 45 minutes to really cater your resume for each job you apply to online. That is a critical step, and that is where you should focus your time.

However, there are times when a company might request a resume and cover letter. Some companies like to ask for a cover letter because they want to evaluate how you write or get your take on how you match the job and your interest level. Or there may be a situation where you are sending your information into a specific company that you want to work inquiring about any openings they might have that match your skills. So cover letters still have their place. Below is what you should do when creating one.

Most jobs have at least a general list of requirements. "Years of experience" may be one of them. Knowing and being proficient on particular software might be another, and so on. You should approach writing a cover letter in a way that allows them to see exactly how well you match the job requirements and preferences they are looking for. A cover letter should list the evidence you have that makes the case that you are perfect for the job. It is your way of proving to an employer that you have everything that they are looking for.

You might be asking, "What is the cover letter supposed to do anyway?" The answer is that it is supposed to increase the curiosity of potential employers enough to motivate them to contact you.

> *A cover letter should increase the curiosity of a potential employer.*

Unlike your resume, where you have a little poetic license or flexibility with grammar and punctuation, your cover letter should be grammatically perfect. Now, assuming that is the case, the format of the cover letter is really the key, as I will explain.

I teach one single way of writing a cover letter, because I have never seen a better way to do it. Plus, the way I teach is completely consistent with the message of this entire book which is again, veterans need to speak the language of corporate America and give employers what they want to see and hear in the format that they are most accustomed to. Vets need to once again step away from all their military training and language and adapt to what civilian employers want. The format for a cover letter you are about to learn does exactly that.

Every cover letter should start off with a few sentences stating your purpose. For example, you should tell them you have applied to their job and list it exactly how they list it. You should tell them that not only are you very interested in the job but that you feel you are a perfect skills match. Then you should tell them you have provided a list of your skills and experience for each of their requirements. So this is how your cover letter may start out:

Dear Mr. Smith,

I am contacting you today to make you aware that I have applied to your Project Management position, job number 1059. Not only am I very interested in the position, but believe I am a perfect skills match. Below, I have provided you a list of my skills and experience for each of your stated job requirements.

From this point you simply make what I like to call a Skills and Experience Comparison Table (SECT). It consists of two columns. The first column is labeled, "Your Requirements." The second column is labeled, "My Skills & Experience."

Now, all you have to do is start listing each of the job requirements they have listed in the job description in column one followed by a brief description of your level of skill or experience that meets or exceeds that requirement in column two. You do this for every requirement they ask for. It will look something like this:

Your Requirements	My Skills & Experience
8-10 years Project Management Experience	10 years of Project Management Experience
Proficient with Microsoft Project	Used Microsoft Project for the last 5 years. Taught an advanced Microsoft Project class at local community college.
Knowledge of Government Procurement Procedures	Worked in Government Procurement Office for 2 years auditing purchasing procedures

After you complete the table, making sure you have addressed each requirement, as well as any of the preferred skills they might ask for, then you are ready for the closing. It should be short, to the point, and include your contact information. For example:

I would sincerely appreciate the opportunity to speak with you about this position. My contact number is 310-555-5555. I will call your office next week to follow up with you.

Sincerely,

Joe Babar

73

Notice how I wrote that I would follow up with him, instead of waiting for him to follow up with me. That is an excellent tactic and very effective. However, you have to give the letter's recipient enough time to receive and read the letter if it was sent by regular mail. Today, most of the time, this can be done via email. Another little trick is to put a read receipt on your email to Mr. Smith to make sure he read your email before you call.

If after a week you not gotten conformation that he has read it, follow up and call him anyway. Remember if you get him on the phone you always can tell him you emailed it to him on a specific day. I have seen hiring managers not read email but then are called and while they are on the phone with the potential candidate, they open and read the email. That is great, and it happened because you followed up. Now, you get a chance to discuss your qualifications. (Caution: Don't be fooled. Any time you are conversing with a company representative, it is an interview. Now, it may not be an official interview but any time you correspond with a company rep by email or in this case over the phone, it might seem like a regular conversation but make no mistake. They are evaluating you so be ready and act accordingly).

Now, some might say that this method only works if there is a job listing that has requirements so you can create the SECT. I would say this method is the most effective if there is a specific job with requirements, but it can still be used for those few times when you might want to target a specific company and are just sending a general inquiry. In those few cases, you can still make a table, but in this case, you would just have one column labeled, "My Skills & Experience" because you don't know what jobs the company has open. Yet the powerful thing about this approach is that you are still letting them know your skill set and how it may match the skill sets they may be looking for.

Speaking realistically, though, if a company doesn't have a specific job opening for you to cater your cover letter toward, this type of general inquiry may be your best bet at getting the employer interested, but it's still a long shot, so please don't spend a lot of time on this approach. I mention it simply because there may be a time when making a general inquiry is the only way of sharing your information with a company that you may be interested in working for. But before you do it, make sure you check out their website to make sure they have no specific job posting that you would be interested in. That is the path of least resistance and that will allow you to use the SECT technique which again is the most effective.

There are many more ways to write a cover letter. There are entire books dedicated to that one subject. But to save you time and a lot of effort, I have given you the one approach I have seen work the best. It is a PROVEN approach. The SECT approach focuses the potential employer reading it on your skills and experience and how well they fit a particular opening they have. This is exactly what you are hoping for. Once they see how well you match the job, they will contact you. This is the exact response are looking for and the reason why you sent them the cover letter in the first place. Give it a try. In those few instances where you need or want to send a cover letter, it will work.

Chapter 8

Networking

The best ways to use your contacts and Social media like Facebook, LinkedIn, Twitter, etc.

Networking is always part of finding a job. For some it is very effective and for others it is marginally effective. The key is to get the word out especially to your friends and family that you are looking for employment and perhaps give them some general information of what you may be looking for. This is just smart and increases your chances of someone hearing about an opening where they work or through their contacts and contacting you.

Many vets feel a little uncomfortable asking their friends and family for help finding a job. I understand. Being a soldier makes a person tougher than the average civilian, better able to take care of himself, and thus, less willing to be a burden on others. Also the reason veterans don't like to ask family and friends for help is because they don't expect or want to be handed anything, but rather, want to earn it on their own through their own merit…just the way they did it in the service. Or soldiers are used to being the protectors, the ones who are keeping their family and friends safe…and thus loathe to have to be on the receiving end for a change. I get it. But actually, every good soldier knows that the mission is the thing, and that sometimes accomplishing the mission requires depending on other people to help you through a tough spot. But if it makes you feel more comfortable, you can just ask them to let you if they hear of any openings. They key is whatever way you want to put it, you need to let them know you are looking, to keep an eye out for you, and ask for their help. A lot of people get hired by leads that friends and relatives have given them. Three of my closest friends contacted me just this year to help them. One of them is a vet. They all got jobs quickly even in this market and all I did was share with them what is in this book and assured them I would keep an eye out for them.

There is an interesting thing that occurs when you ask your friends and family to keep an eye out for you. You create a group of people who are motivated to help you. Instead of you just looking for a job, now you have many people. This is important in a challenging job market. You want as many people helping you as you can get. Plus these people, your friends and family, are most likely to take an extra step or two when they hear of an opening that might interest you. It is smart. Just Do It.

> *Networking is always a part of finding a job. The key is to get the word out that you are looking for employment.*

Another thing about networking is what you do on your own at meetings or events. For example, if you go to a job fair, a club or organization meeting, make it a habit of collecting business cards. These are your contacts. These are you leads. When you get a business card from anyone, you should email them within 24 hours with your resume and past performance review and just tell them it was nice meeting them and tell them you are looking for full time employment. Then just ask them to please let you know if they hear of anything. It is that simple and it is REALLY effective.

Now, some may feel a little uncomfortable with sending their past performance review to someone they just met. Once again, I understand. But people emailing a resume to someone they met is common. But someone sending a resume and their past performance review is not common. It peaks the interest of the person you are sending it to. It increases their curiosity and they will most likely read it and your resume. Plus even if they don't personally have any openings, after you motivated them to read both your resume and performance evaluation, if they know of someone who does have an opening, they are most likely going to just hit the "Forward" key and send that person (who has an opening) both your resume and past performance review. You win. This is exactly what you wanted, and it was all because you followed up quickly on your networking opportunities and you went that one extra step.

Now, the subject of Social Networking or Social Media like Facebook, LinkedIn, Twitter, etc.. More and more companies are using these avenues but it might not be in the way you think. I hear more and more every day that companies use, for example, someone's Facebook page to screen them. You would not believe what some people post on their Facebook page that can be considered a deal breaker for a company interested in considering them for a job. I have seen it happen time and time again. So please listen carefully: take everything off your Facebook, MySpace, and Twitter page that you would not want to share with any potential employer. For instance, most of us would know we shouldn't have pictures of last Halloween where we wore a lampshade and our boxer shorts, but keep religious and political views or affiliations off as well. This is not about limiting your freedom of speech or religion, it is about getting you a job. Then go in and change your privacy settings to ensure that only those that have your permission get to see your information.

Don't make the mistake of saying to yourself, "I don't need to take anything down. I will adjust my privacy settings so only the people I 'friend' can see my information." That might seem like a solution, but what if a hiring manager or recruiter sends you a "friend" request? Then what? And yes, company reps do this. So first, take everything down, and then adjust your privacy settings.

I want to caution you also about the amount of time you feel you need to spend on these Social Networking sites. Yes, you should let people know, especially your friends and family, that you are looking for full-time employment. But that doesn't mean that you should spend six hours a day updating your Facebook page either. Too many people think that they are going to find a job on one of these sites and they spend hours and hours on them. That is a mistake. Even LinkedIn, which seems to be geared to more professional pursuits, can drain you of a lot of job searching time for little reward.

Now, I don't want you to think that I'm against Social Networking; I'm not. But it is just one tool you should be using in your job search. You need to spend most of your time on finding openings, catering your resume to those openings, and getting prepared for the interview. Those are the critical steps. Social Networking is not, at least not at this point in time.

As time goes on, the social networking sites might become more and more important in your job search. There might be a time where they offer more and more ways of making job searches easier and more effective. But for now, it is just a small part of your total job search so please adjust the time you spend on them, at least for finding a job, to the appropriate level.

Chapter 9

Final Tips, Thoughts, and Advice

Assorted advice to help you get hired.

First, I want to provide you with my email address if you have questions, comments or success stories. Feel free to contact me at:

Mark@DoThisGetHired.com

Please include your name, rank, branch of service, and how many years you were in.

Use this book as a reference.

If you don't think you are getting the results you want in the time you want it, go back and read specific chapters again. I don't expect you to retain every piece of information, but what I have learned is that those few candidates that are not having the success they were looking for, are only implementing some of the advice from a certain chapters. In other words, their implementation of those techniques I have provided them are incomplete. The simple solution is to just review, from time to time, the advice I have provided, to ensure you're implementing all of it.

Be patient.

The job search is a process that takes some time. You should be prepared for that. Yes the advice you have just read has helped some people get hired very quickly and others it has taken a number of weeks. The

important thing is that you stay focused and stick with the techniques you
have learned. They will help you get hired as quickly as possible.

Keep trying.
I know it is hard not to have a job. I know the stress it causes for both
the person looking and their families. That is one of the main reasons I
wrote this book; to help vets find employment.   And it has helped many
so now it is your turn.

Don't expect to find your dream job right away.
Please adjust your expectations and understand that you might have to
take a job you *like* and work there for a year or two before you get the job
you love.

If you're qualified, apply.
Apply to every job you qualify for, as opposed to only the jobs you like
the most. This is very important. Again, sometimes getting started or
getting your foot in the door is the most important step towards you
getting the job you really love.

Keep your geographical location open.
Too many times I have talked to vets that only want to stay in one
particular part of the country and don't look anywhere else. That is a
huge mistake because you are greatly reducing the number of jobs that
are available to you.

Oftentimes, moving away today doesn't mean you'll have to remain gone
forever. Let's say you want to stay in your home state. But you apply for
a job with a company, which, although it has operations in your home
state, are just not hiring there right now, but they are hiring in another
state. What if you took that job in another state for two years, and then
something opened back up in your come state and you could relocate
back? Would that be worth the two years away? The point is, try to get
yourself into the mindset of, *I will take a job wherever there is a good
opportunity.* Then, once you have the job and have worked in it for a
couple of years, you can come up with a plan to try to work your way
into a position back in your home state.

Chapter 9: Final Tips, Thoughts, and Advice

Remember that when you have a job, it is easier and a lot less pressure to find another one. I understand that there are all things to consider when leaving. Like your family and extended family and how far away they will be. But if you get a good job, that pays you a good salary, you'll have the money to go visit and/or bring your family to you for a visit. Please, please find a way to open up your geographical preferences. The job market for vets is just too challenging for you to limit yourself geographically.

Thank you again for your great service to our country. Now, together, let's get you a job.

When you have success and you get a job, please email me at Mark@DoThisGetHired.com with your story and how my advice helped you. I would like to use this feedback to help other vets get hired and it is really helpful to get some personal stories to share from fellow vets and service members.

You can find more information about the book and me at www.DoThisGetHired.com or on Amazon.com.

19.99

CPSIA information can be obtained at www.ICGtesting.com
Printed in the USA
LVOW121747121011

250222LV00001B/206/P

9 781456 496128